MY PILLOW

GOLF ON
MY PILLOW

Midnight letters to
a son in foreign parts
from

GEORGE HOUGHTON

a Golf Addict
—who also did the drawings

STANLEY PAUL

London

STANLEY PAUL & CO. LTD
178–202 Great Portland Street, London, W.1

AN IMPRINT OF THE   HUTCHINSON GROUP

London Melbourne Sydney
Auckland Bombay Toronto
Johannesburg New York

First published 1958

Second Impression 1959

This edition 1960

*This book has been printed in Great Britain by
litho-offset at Taylor Garnett Evans & Co. Ltd.,
Watford, Herts, and bound by them*

TO KAY

"Quick! let's drive off before it rains .."

A NOTE TO GOLF ADDICTS

THESE letters about golf were written to my son when he was overseas in a land where there are neither fairways nor fair ladies.

Golf is in the lad's blood. He is addicted by heritage and it consoles me to think that if I give him nothing else he hasn't done so badly. A boy's best friend is his par.

My son says he enjoyed receiving the letters. I had fun writing them. All that remains—now that they are offered as a book—is that you also should be interested, particularly if you are a cash customer!

Some say that addicts like talking, listening, and reading golf, as much as they like playing. I am counting on that.

As you would expect, I have edited and supplemented the letters. Also, my sketches have been added to cheer the book up. However, in the main, this is what I believe a golf-starved young man in the Middle East would want. Of course, I hope you don't have to be golf-starved, *and* in the Middle East, before you can find something you like in *Golf on my Pillow*.

As an addict, you will not agree with all my theories, and I am quite sure that the stories and experiences are no better than many in your own stock. But if my notes serve to stimulate and jog your memory, so much the better. The book will have served a good purpose.

'Golf on my Pillow' was chosen as a title because most of the letters were written in bed while normal people sleep. Also, come to think of it, when I play good golf it is usually on those smooth fairways of dreamland.

George Houghton

DEAR SON: Thank you for your letter. So now you have arrived at the desert outpost, *sans* comfort, *sans* golf, *sans* everything. . . .

Your request that my letters be mainly about golf pleased me. This indicates that you have reached man's estate and your sense of values is keenly developed.

I shall do as you ask. At regular intervals, while the rest of the world sleeps and everything is nice and quiet, I shall jot down random thoughts about our wonderful game. Thus I shall keep you up to date in the important things. Others can attend to family news.

Somerset Maugham once said that reading about cards and bridge enables one to bear a bad cold in the head with patience, and a peremptory demand for income tax with fortitude. Personally, I derive solace from golf books, so I understand how letters on the subject can well bring pleasant thoughts to your desert—maybe even a whiff of newly mown fairway.

It is past midnight, but I feel full of good common sense. I am not tired. Just the opposite in fact, and were I to find myself at this moment out on the first tee I am quite sure I could put up a wonderful performance.

The reasons for my slice—a chronic affliction—are crystal clear. I know why shots through the green kick to the right; why long putts never quite make it. . . . Tonight, all that could be put right.

This kind of intelligence I shall try to pass on, hoping that even while you are *hors de golf* your game may retain its vigour.

In any case, the asides about other people's play are important (to them!) and will greatly add to your fun.

Perhaps you have guessed that at this moment I am still glowing from what could be described as a near magnificent round of golf.

Five successive bogeys are never bad, and I am quite sure that even you, with the strong courage of youth and a pretty pivot, would also have enjoyed my experience.

Most unfortunately, after this pleasant spell, I sclaffed my drive into long grass (where you expect to find bodies), took eight to get into the last hole, and finally finished the round twelve over fours.

Things might have been so different. Had the eight been a five, had I not stupidly driven out of bounds at the fourth, and approached so badly to four greens. . . . Then, my dear boy, your ageing parent would have returned a gross seventy! You remember that the great Robert D'Arcy Locke could do no better than a seventy-two when he played our course.

So near was I to greatness.

Looking back, I would say that the finest round of golf I ever played—level threes at St. Andrews—took place after a Golf Society dinner. Bedded and secure, I was spending the night in my London club, comfortable enough to enjoy every second of that delicious dream. It will always be one of my happiest golfing memories.

The opponent on this occasion was young Peter Thomson. He also had a good round. We were engaged in the play-off for the British Open, or maybe it was the World Open. I've forgotten.

There were thousands of spectators. Those from my home club, all looking like Mephistopheles—hoping I would miss every putt. But I didn't. The ball dropped from all angles, sometimes even when I exploded from bunkers.

The weather, I remember, was strange even for Scotland—snow, with tropical sunshine. Although the greens were concrete hard, I was constantly getting deep suckers on the fairways. . . .

It was a match of thrills. Having actually holed out with a shot played from the Swilcan Burn, I went on to perform in a manner which caused old Willie Auchterlonie to raise his eyebrows. I don't think he had ever seen anything like it.

There are hazards, even in dreamland, but when my ball plugged itself firmly in the face of Hell Bunker it seemed the most natural thing in the world to take a blaster, face in the opposite direction to the green, and play a full shot, scooping the ball right over my head on to the fairway. My drive at the Road Hole landed and stopped, in some miraculous fashion, right on top of the shed. I elected to play it, explaining to my mystified caddie that a number four wood was designed for that very shot.

The exciting drama ended with a presentation of a gold cup which someone filled with champagne. I think it was the sight of this which awoke me. As well it might, for my friends at dinner had filled my glass too often. . . .

Nearly all my brilliant golf has been played in dreamland. If only I could reproduce the magnificent shots which I play on my pillow! The sideboard would sag with cups and salvers. Hogan, Thomson, Locke, and Rees would bite finger nails, and clamour for a revision of their handicaps.

Writing of St. Andrews reminds me of the great Andrew Kirkaldy, a dour Scottish giant who has now gone through to play on Elysian Fields. His golf was smooth as silk, although his tongue was rough as a rasp.

Andra was employed as permanent professional to the Royal and Ancient—no man can attain more—and over the years tales about him have produced millions of good belly laughs. I'm not thinking only of the naughty stories—like the one which also concerns the Bishop of London—but of the apt retorts, credited to Andrew, which have served to immortalize his memory.

Now, I'm going to tell you of another Kirkaldy—Bill Kirkaldy, a near neighbour and friend.

In 1928 Bill was captain of England at a game called hockey; also, he was North of England champion at squash, and a fairly regular performer at Wimbledon. . . . But there is a much more important aspect of his sporting prowess. It would be accurate to say that, but for some tragic diversion in the stream of circumstance, Bill could have been a golfer. Maybe one of the greats.

What do you think of this?

In the twenties, when my friend was always in the sporting headlines with his hockey, squash, tennis, and such, he acquired a bag of golf sticks, and happily hacked his way through odd week-ends perhaps three or four times a year. After a while he must have been cracking them sweetly enough, for he decided that golf was a pretty good game. Not that he had much time himself, but it would be nice for young Tim, his twelve-year-old son.

So Bill had a Professional cut down his hickory clubs to fit Tim, and the lad got started. That was a long time ago and we have no evidence that young T. ever persevered with the game. Which was a pity, for he went on to become British public-schools' light-weight boxing champion, and an efficient performer at other games too.

Years slipped quietly away, and it would not appear that Bill Kirkaldy even gave a thought to golf. Then, one day he was invited to play for a scratch side of business associates against a team representative of the British Press. Decidedly a social affair. High-level golf was hardly called for, but good manners, sociability, and straight drives (to avoid too much irritating ball-hunting) were obviously the order of the day.

Bill hadn't played for years, but under the stairs he found an old bag of clubs, so set off with a song in his heart for the Edgbaston golf course. It was a lovely summer morning with the whole world smiling. His chosen opponent was on the editorial staff of the *Financial Times*. A good player.

Before starting, the contestants sucked in hot coffee, with lots of rum and bonhomie. Then they took their turn on the first tee. Bill teed up and addressed his ball. Friends may or may not have noticed that his usual cheery smile had faded to a pale, strained

expression. This was not surprising. With a mighty shock, Bill had just discovered that the clubs in his old bag were the dwarf appliances which had been cut down for young Tim!

No one on the tee—and there were a dozen waiting players—commented on Bill's equipment. It just isn't done. After all, some folk have interesting foibles, such as looking at the ball with the left eye only, or breathing in deeply before starting to pivot. In tournaments Max Faulkner sometimes has ladies' clubs. And so on. . . . The onlookers surely decided that the kind of equipment a player uses is entirely his own affair, and no doubt by trial and error the chap on the tee had discovered that short shafts suited him. But it *was* queer. . . .

How did Bill get on? Well, he was too flabbergasted at the start to say a word. The man must have nerves of steel, for his first drive went long and straight. And that was his undoing, for after hitting the ball a real purler how could he explain to his pleasant opponent that he was, in fact, playing under a very severe handicap? I don't know full details of how the game went, but I do know that Bill defeated his man 3 and 2.

They had nice drinks in the bar. Bill's prestige was terrific. He didn't comment on his Lilliputian golf clubs. It would have been like saying, 'How much easier I could have beaten you with decent equipment!' But although Bill kept mum, his opponent had plenty to say about the clubs. To the entire company he told the story of Bill's astonishing play: '—And did you see the sort of clubs he uses? Hickories, cut down!'

Can't you just imagine the faraway look coming into their eyes as they muttered, 'There may be something in this short-shaft idea. . . .'

I asked Bill Kirkaldy if he ever played with the clubs again.

He looked slightly ashamed. 'No,' he said, 'as a matter of fact my wife used them for the chrysanthemums!'

You shall have another letter soon.

Yours,
DAD

2

DEAR SON: Tonight, as I shiver under four blankets, with another over my shoulders to make sitting up in bed possible, I think of you stewing in the heat. My breath is like smoke, even in the bedroom, but although it must have been colder on the golf course this afternoon, I scarcely noticed. Frost was in the air and no doubt my set of woods were glad that I had recently bought them nice warm covers! Yet we were glowing and happy, and the golf, while poorish in execution, was pleasant.

With my friend John Hynd, and two twin brothers named Grubb—as alike as two peas—we played on a Middlesex course called Whitewebs.

John is a Member of Parliament. In the Attlee Government he was Chancellor of the Duchy of Lancaster and Minister responsible for the administration of Germany and Austria. Being a Scot, he naturally turns to golf when political duties become irksome. Mostly it is pure relaxation but twice a year he plays serious stuff with the Parliamentary Golfing Society at Walton Heath. He was telling me how he once partnered Lord Saltoun, who is worth a paragraph in anyone's golf book. The worthy peer plays with one of those extraordinary clubs with an all-purpose, adjustable head. He arrives on the tee, equipped as he likes to be, with one solitary club and the small square kind of attaché-case in which British workmen sometimes carry their midday snacks. The little bag doesn't rattle, so perhaps it contains waterproofs. Nevertheless, Lord Saltoun usually hits them down the middle, seldom

15

off the fairway, and to be able to count on that every time I know plenty of golfers who would risk looking like plumbers.

John Hynd usually plays at Whitewebs. The course is so called because an extraordinary phenomena of nature occurs during a certain season of each year. Queer insects cause fine skeins of silver web to cover the grass. Sometimes the distance looks so white that a red ball seems essential.

The ground is clay, and heavier than most. In fact, our shoes had soles nearly two inches thick with mud, clinging like plasticine. In consequence, our standard of play was indifferent, in marked contrast to the company which was excellent. Over the course there winds a stream where John Hynd, with a long scoop, once salvaged no fewer than thirty-six golf balls!

All my life I have opposed the bringing of dogs on to golf courses. This afternoon, since I was a guest, there was nothing I could say. But imagine my horror when I discovered that John, with whom I had never previously played, is *always* accompanied by his fine red setter! My attitude will not change, but never have

I seen, nor am I ever likely to see, such a well-trained animal. Not only does Rufus freeze, statue-like, while a player addresses his ball, but he actually finds the ball, and awaits the striker. He never walks on ahead, always skirts the greens, and all in all behaves better than most spectators and many golfers I know. All that remains is for this intelligent animal to be taught to swing a golf club and John will have made a valuable contribution to the golfing scene.

So, while you sweltered under a mosquito net for a midday siesta, we glowed and purred at the close of a pleasant round of golf in almost Arctic conditions.

Our start having been delayed, we did not reach John's house for lunch until about three o'clock. Mrs. Hynd, reasonably cordial, was in the doorway. We apologized for being late.

'Being a golfer's wife has its drawbacks,' I said. 'One of them is a tendency to wait for meals. . . .'

Mrs. Hynd smiled. 'I'm the best heater-up of lunches in the South of England,' she said.

Golf addicts less fortunate than I, know the agonies of wife trouble. Many a good medal card has been wrecked on the last few holes because 'luncheon anxiety' has set in. Middle iron shots are the first to be affected. You hurry them. Then, as you start to get your excuses for being late ready, your concentration wobbles, and all the other clubs turn to sticks of asparagus. Your game goes to pot, and it would be true to say that the round was wrecked on your front porch before you left home.

The golfer setting off for a Sunday morning four-ball who makes a promise to his wife that he will be home for lunch at a fixed time, is a fool. He may either break his word, or neglect the ritual of drinks at the bar.

The latter is important. Not merely because it is pleasant to regurgitate well-chewed morsels of golf gossip, but also it is a duty to listen while a brother addict holds the floor. These chaps all have to listen to you, so keep quiet and let them have a turn.

The most difficult thing about golf is learning not to talk about it. But that is half the fun and such pleasant causerie must not be

"Dare you to take on this gal!"

curtailed because some woman awaits with a hot meal. The greatest blight on golf could well be the single sentence, 'Don't be later than one o'clock!'

Perfection at our great game is forged in the roaring furnace of self-criticism, patience, humility, and often enough, domestic turmoil. So, my boy, when you take a wife, see she has sympathy for the game. Unless she is a golfer it is unlikely that she will know that cheese and pickles at three o'clock often taste better than saddle of mutton with veg. at one-thirty.

There are three kinds of wives. Your selection must be obvious. The terror, who plays merry Hades every Sunday when you are late for lunch; the woman golfer, who understands, but insists on nattering golf instead of doing the housework.

Finally, there is the jewel of great value. Like Mrs. John Hynd, she accepts her fate, becoming an expert heater-up of Sunday lunches.

Yours,
DAD

"—And that's a seven iron shot!"

DEAR SON: Two or three days in Scotland—with the full treatment! Let me tell you about it.

First, on Friday evening, a sweet eighteen holes with Peter (maker-of-wonderful-golf-shoes) Norwell, on the Rosemount course at Blairgowrie—in my opinion one of the six most beautiful terrains in the world. On Saturday, I watched the thirty-six holes final of the Amateur at St. Andrews, and was lucky enough to be standing at the edge of the long, narrow twelfth green when Joe Carr's 360 yard drive landed. He holed the putt for an eagle!

Then, a spring-chicken dinner at the home of the respected and venerable club-maker, Tom Auchterlonie. We discussed his craft.

'If you ask me,' said the maestro, 'youngsters with wedges are just gravediggers. When I see them taking up deep divots of our lovely turr-r-f it hurts me like pulling a tooth. . . .'

On the Sabbath morn', boy Eric, who efficiently manages the business for his father, took me to play the Balcomie Links, near Crail. Here is a grand seaside club which claims seventh place in the table of seniority: Royal Burgess (1735), Honourable Company of Edinburgh Golfers (1744), Royal and Ancient (1754), Bruntsfield (1761), Royal Musselburgh (1774), and Royal Aberdeen (1780). Balcomie was established in 1786.

I got the full story from a proud member who told how 'the ancient burghers of Crail were introduced to the game by mer-

This could well be the one I've waited years for...

TEE THOUGHTS NO. 1

chants from the Netherlands who called at the Port . . .' Golf from Holland? I know a few who would dispute that!

And so to the mecca. I get so furious with those insensitive, granite-hearted, cockle-eyed dullards who cannot appreciate the best things in life, and attempt to criticize the Old Course at St. Andrews. All this blather about unfair hidden hazards, and bunkers turned the wrong way round. . . .

I could not deal adequately with the critics, but I know who could—and do!

The six elders who sit at the table in the big bay-window of the R. and A. clubhouse look down like Tibetan priests, gravely watching poor sinners (non-members) striving for absolution on the first tee.

I've had drinks with these Royals and Ancients. The sense of

"This is the Swilcan Burn — it's caused more trouble than the Battle of Bannockburn!"

superiority you get while sitting at that exposed table is positively amazing. 'The Sages' would make a wonderful subject for a painter. The picture should be commissioned without delay, for changes are coming, and some of us who like things as they are, will want to be reminded of that window.

The picture could hang till eternity alongside the full-length Orpen painting of the Prince of Wales. The latter, with grand portraits of Freddy Tait, Tom Morris, and others, hangs in the main room. Like the others, it is now a period piece. Zig-zag pullover, plus fours, and an enormous flat cap—His Royal Highness, at twenty-two years of age, stands on the course looking pensive, as if his ball has just skirted Lions Mouth bunker, bounced over the Cat's Trap, and is probably in the Coffins. . . .

The bunkers at St. Andrews are more intimately known than any in the world. Each of the hundred famous ones has a name and a clearly defined personality. I learnt about them from a great authority.

Carnegie Grant is 176 lb. and fifty-four years of pure caddie. He is one of the twelve who are licensed at St. Andrews. Carnegie has been doing this important job since he left school. Second in command to the famous 'Tip' Anderson, and with the possible exception of Tip, Carnegie knows more about the Old Course at St. Andrews than any living man.

Carnegie knew the great Andra Kirkaldy ('Och, my faether's pit him t' bed monny a time'). He is conscientious, skilled, and friendly.

'Bunkers are no' what they were in the auld days,' says Grant, and went on to explain how the new flat-soled, sand-blaster clubs have 'removed the sting'.

But although folk don't spend so much time in the bunkers it doesn't mean they play the course quicker. If there is anything that Carnegie deplores it is slow play. He told me how, in 1922, Jock Hutchison beat the American Joe Kirkwood 4 and 3—taking 74 shots and one hour and twenty minutes to complete the round!

Carnegie knows it all. He remembers, when Mr. Angus Hambro was made Captain of the R. and A., the first and last holes were illuminated with lanterns and motor-car headlights. Four members played a two-hole match at midnight before a thousand spectators. The first hole was won in bogey, and the eighteenth halved in fives.

I tell Carnegie Grant that with a name like his he should have been Prime Minister. He is not amused. 'Jist keep your eye on the ball, sir,' he says, and points out the direction. He has it taped, and coming home, from the twelfth tee, he aims you at St. Regulus Tower, College Tower, Hope Park Church, the tall chimneys, or the 'wee white hoose', depending not only on the hole you are playing, but on his assessment of your capabilities. His accuracy is unerring and I only wish I could 'Jist put yersel' in my hands, sir' more often.

The Crescent, the Beardies, Hell's Kitchen, the Cat Trap, Rab's Bunker, Principal's Nose, Grant's, Kruger, and Mrs. Kruger. . . . Carnegie knows every bunker. He knows that Strath, on the 7th, has wrecked more cards than almost any other. It was named after David Strath, young Tom Morris's great rival. I put my tee shot plump into the middle of it, went through the usual routine of failing with my first attempt, then blasted too big with my second. . . . 'Your performance is no' unique,' consoled my caddie.

Carnegie remembered the Open of 1921 when Hutchison almost holed the 9th in one. A spectator ran on to the green and tugged out the flag. The ball slowly trickled over the hole!

The 11th, about 165 yards, has often been 'aced', but also there have been tragedies. Once, two players halved the hole in eighteen. And that was in an Amateur Championship! Bobby Jones met his doom here in the 1921 Open. His tee shot was bunkered, he failed twice, then blasted so hard that his fourth went into the Eden River.

Well, the good Carnegie Grant can tell you all these things. He was caddying for Cyril Tolley in 1925 when that mighty man drove the 18th green three times. Think of it, 360 yards in one wallop with a hickory-shafted club!

And now, I am back from St Andrews and trying to live it all again on my pillow, passing on to you the highlights. Maybe we shall soon be playing the Old together again in a grand all-male fourball. What a pleasant thought . . .

I have been thinking about my last letter to you.

Am I giving the impression that I am a woman-hater? Heaven forbid! *Tantœne animis cœlestibus irœ?* No. At this precise moment my wrath takes a different turn.

Some golfers, many of them, alas, professionals, are creating rumpi which should have no place in our peaceful game. I shall tell you what is on my mind and hope that you also feel this way.

First of all, while admiring proficiency, I do not believe that the actual striking of the ball is the most important thing in golf. Really great golfers usually hold similar views, although additionally they seem to strike the ball surprisingly well.

When three elderly, happy hackers invite a Professional to make up a four-ball you then have a situation which can decide the whole story of good behaviour on a golf course. At any rate, you can assess the calibre of the Professional. If he regards his eighteen handicap partner as an important member of the side, if he enjoys gentle leg-pulls with the others . . . In other words, if he enters completely into the spirit of a pleasant game (even if he has to spend half the morning looking for balls) then, my son, this chap is not only a good club Professional but is entitled to be called a golfer.

On the other hand, if the paid member of the four-ball oozes condescension and regards every fluffed shot with a smelt-manure expression. . . . Be he the world's best striker of golf balls, I still regard him unworthy of the honourable title.

No two golf courses are even remotely alike. This also applies to golfers. It is extraordinary that the things which we hate most in others are often faults peculiarly our own. You know what I mean: Explaining to an opponent, who couldn't care less, exactly what went wrong when you had a bad shot; repeating: 'I can't understand it. I'm not usually off my game like this. . . .'

But these waffles are not half so bad as disagreeing with an opponent who has been kind enough to say 'Good shot' after you have played. That is the limit! The ball has been struck as well as

It's really all a question of Geometry!

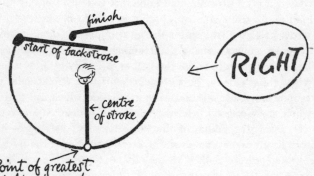

finish

start of backstroke

RIGHT ←

← centre of stroke

Point of greatest clubhead speed

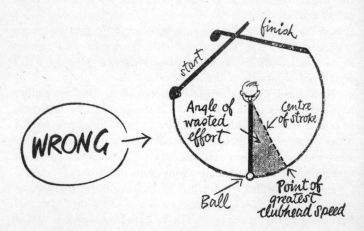

WRONG →

start

finish

Angle of wasted effort

Centre of stroke →

Ball

Point of greatest clubhead speed

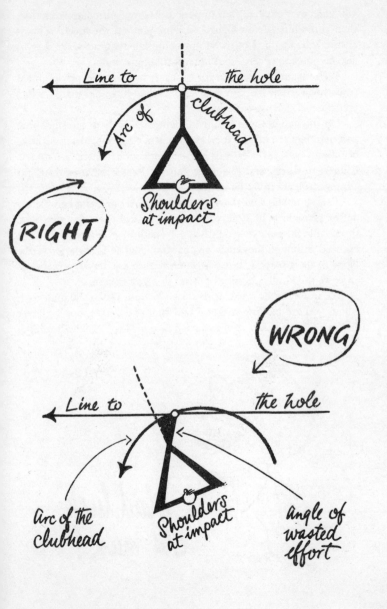

you need ever expect, your opponent has murmured appreciation, then you whine 'A bit short,' or 'Not *quite* off the meat.' This is always infuriating. Let us accept compliments graciously. Let us also be quick to praise—but in truthful moderation.

We must not forget that the quickest way to make an opponent reach for a lethal weapon is to say, 'O, bad luck, old man'—when your face is radiant with joy.

On the golf courses in our verdant islands there are signs that bad manners are on the increase. This is a serious, alarming state of affairs which calls for corrective action where necessary. Chinese tortures and the rack can no longer be used but our admonishments must be no less severe.

Tantrums show weakness. Also they are a bore, and completely out of place in golf. Folk who cannot control their tongues, who throw things, behave stupidly . . . should never completely be excused, although they may 'beg pardon' loud and long afterwards. None of us is perfect, but wherever else we err, let us preserve at all costs the kindly dignities proper to a golf course.

We must not be weak at the crisis points. When the man with whom you are playing makes a bad shot and *laughs*, don't glower and reach for a heavy iron to smash into his skull. Like all scratch

"O, bad luck old man!"

golfers we must be prepared to meet golf on equal terms, but peacefully.

Slander the Government, curse the income-tax man, blast your butcher, baker, or ballistic-missile maker, but bite off your tongue rather than mutter a bad-natured gripe 'twixt first tee and eighteenth green. Even extend your good manners to the clubhouse.

I would not say that the following comes under the heading 'Bad Manners', but if the statement is true then maybe some outbursts should be excused. These extraordinary lines were penned by Dr. A. S. Lamb from the sanctum of the great McGill University, in the United States.

Golf increases the blood pressure, ruins the disposition, spoils the digestion, induces neurasthenia, hurts the eyes, callouses the hands, ties kinks in the nervous system, debauches the morals, drives men to drink or homicide, breaks up the family, turns the ductless glands into internal warts, corrodes the pneumogastric nerves, breaks off the edges of the vertebrae, induces spinal meningitis, and progressive mendacity, and starts angina pectoris.

I don't believe it.

Yours,
DAD

DEAR SON: Thank you for your letter. I am glad that my golf notes are making you want to get cracking, despite the heat.

Your difficulties in laying out even a simple pitch and putt course are fully appreciated. It must be irritating to know that a shot decent enough to go any distance nearly always results in the loss of a ball by thieving natives. I can picture them hiding behind clumps of camel thorn and pouncing on your ball rather as they do on an egg when it is released from one of their tired chickens.

Having much experience with these people, it is not necessary for me to ask why they steal golf balls. It is quite certain that they are not used for their correct purpose. Perhaps the thief bores holes through them for beads, but more than likely the whole operation is simply to indulge their inherent passion for stealing. The necessity for periodical searches of the native village is appreciated, and I suppose rounding up contraband arms is as good an excuse as any.

Should you decide to continue with the idea of making a golf course on your bit of desert, it may be helpful if I tell you how certain British golf addicts in West Africa have overcome difficulties even greater than yours.

At Mpraeso, near Mount Adnamsa, the highest peak in the territory, a certain Mr. Bill Adams who is a Government Agent, has made what he terms 'a three-hole convertible'. Here, in fact, is a splendid little golf course cut from the dense forest. The actual cutting, which must not be neglected whenever the tropical rains permit, does not involve gang-mowers and such. It is a relentless axe-battle against a growth, which, if left for a month, would engulf the course completely. On one occasion Bill's absence put normal maintenance out of gear. On return he had the greatest difficulty in finding where the course had been!

Please do not imagine that golf at Mpraeso is played in jest. The terrain is situated on the way from Accra to Kumasi, in the heart of the Ashanti kingdom. The air is good up there and it ought to be, for you are 2,200 feet above sea level.

As explained, there are only three greens, but a variety of tees set at varying angles make nine completely different holes. The grass is lush and soft, but the actual holes have a 'surround' of smooth concrete. Folk make good use of the course, and what they lack in numbers perhaps they make up for in quality. Four or five very nice chaps in fact.

I am glad to say that at Mpraeso there is no shortage of caddies, which is just as well, for they are necessary to keep the snakes at bay.

So you see, Bill Adams and his friends, despite difficulties, have been able to answer the clarion call. I am quite sure that in your next letter you will tell me how your bulldozers have levelled off the escarpment, and how military police dogs have been trained to safeguard your precious stock of golf balls. . . .

You makers of courses can never get a just reward. Unfortunately, but usually, grumbles and complaints are heaped upon you. Once in a while you and your committee will get a collective vote of thanks at the Annual General Meeting, but nearly always your heads will be bowed with the plaintive protests of members who have a habit of expecting perfection in all things.

Sometimes complaints are justified. At the Nyanza Club, at Kisuma, on the Kasat river in Kenya, pressure from members resulted in the following being printed on the back of the score-card:

31

If a ball come to rest in dangerous proximity to a hippopotamus or crocodile, another ball may be dropped at a safe distance, no nearer the hole, without penalty.

You will admit that this state of affairs is even more irritating than having your golf balls stolen by Arabs!

Nevertheless, I firmly believe that such difficulties fade to insignificance compared with the psychological problems facing all golfers everywhere, always.

Good golf, although beautiful, is such a sensitive thing. The game has been well described as 'fugitive'.

Take the case of Bill Corbett.

Bill is an extremely agreeable young man who claims his greatest weakness is he 'bruises too quick'. He is the Professional at the Castlewood Country Club, in the United States. Some do not believe that Americans have the same sensitive, easily damaged feelings that the average English bloke has to endure. This is a fallacy. Golf makes jellyfish of us all, no matter what race or creed.

The whole world should know about Bill. In an important cash tournament his figures for three rounds were 69, 89, 69. What went wrong on the second day? *His wife presented him with a lovely baby girl!*

Consider this. A knowledgeable operator, whose easy skill you would imagine to be unassailable, gets knocked for a Burton by a not unusual domestic occurrence. After all, he is only required to continue steadily hitting a small golf ball into a hole—a habit he has thoroughly acquired—yet he is easily thrown off balance.

Bill Corbett plays three rounds of golf. Twice he is four shots inside par; the other round he plays like a long-handicap dub. One would expect that Bill's background of tournament experience would give him complete immunity from outside distractions. In the normal way he plays golf almost instinctively. Almost, but not quite. A mental disturbance snaps something inside, muscles don't respond, and he flounders. In fact, he takes just twenty strokes more than he should, which is probably rather worse than you or I would do.

"Quiet dear, while I'm putting..."

Mind over matter. With golf it is ever thus. That is why—if we *must* play on top form *always*—a course of mind training is essential. The only alternative is to fill ourselves full of dope so that our minds simply don't exist.

There is not a golfer in the whole wide world who cannot appreciate the purgatory of Corbett's second round. In varying degrees we have all similarly suffered. Bill knew quite well what he must do, but couldn't. He has played the allowed number of shots for a hole, perhaps one more. . . . But the ball is still sitting up, grinning at him. The sustained agony of having to keep on tapping the damned thing until it finally does the death rattle in the cup! No torture can beat that.

Putters' pangs, the dreaded twitch. . . . Bill had the lot. Most of his shots were lost on the greens, where non-golfers think there are neither hazards nor difficulties (I can hear your hollow laughter). No doubt after missing a few short ones, Bill took longer and longer for his putts. . . . Every blade of grass was carefully examined, the bent ones straightened. . . . Painstaking care—perhaps. But I believe Bill was merely putting off the dreaded moment when he must actually tap the ball.

There are golfers who play every day and endure this sort of

Ten to one this goes in the wood . . .
Oooo...

TEE THOUGHTS NO. 2

agony at least once a month. They give up 'the damn fool game' at tea-time, but by first light next morning are out on the lawn practising chip shots.

Golf is said to be a practical solution to satisfy every natural tendency to get into trouble. This is a high-falutin way of putting it, but we would agree that golf courses are all battlefields.

You stand on the first tee and you are a parachutist awaiting the order to drop. The terrain is impregnated with danger. Unknown difficulties await, but there is no turning back. Your brain is addled by an instructor's last-minute advice. You brace for action, and the battle begins.

Sometimes it helps to see comrades in trouble around you. It is consolation to know that they also are vulnerable. . . . You have been schooled in bravery, so calculated risk is normal routine. But also you must be prudent. It is the final objective that counts— whether it is a first-class medal round, or merely the annihilation of an enemy.

Victory at any cost? That is a question always asked, whether the battle be fought with guns, or golf clubs, brawn, or brains. You fight to win for self-preservation?—Or because you like the fun of conflict?

Writing of Bill Corbett reminds me of another American. He is also a very skilled operator.

Phil Galvano has his golf academy in the street of the honky-tonks, right in the heart of night-club land, on 52nd Street, right-hand side, walking towards Broadway. Practically none of Phil's neighbours open their businesses until late at night. But Phil starts early. It was 9.30 a.m. when I called to make an appointment, but a well-known dance-band leader was already in a lather of perspiration at the nets.

Like Ernest Jones, Galvano has brought to golf some unorthodox ideas. Jones preaches one fundamental theme and insists that the whole game is fantastically simple. On the other hand, Phil Galvano has ferreted out some rather complicated scientific theories resultant from deep research. Ballistics, mathematics, and even medicine, have all been included in Phil's studies.

First of all, take the short game. Phil is an apostle of the 'Master Eye' theory, whereby you must discover, either by consulting an optician, or in another way which Phil can explain to you himself, which of your eyes gives 'correct central fixation'. The Master Eye can give you a direct line of vision, while the 'depth eye' searches out an angle which meets at the focal point. . . . And so on. Then, there is the important question of 'right-angled vision', but here again Phil must explain that to you himself—if you have time when you are in New York. He may also teach you the seven exercises which you can do (even in bed at night, or in the office) to establish a sound 'putting gaze'.

Still on putting. Phil Galvano is a brilliant exponent. He favours the cradle motion—arms bent outwards with elbows pointing in direction line—wrists bent, but with 'frozen hinges'. This technique is not so very uncommon for putting, but Phil also advocates it for chipping, and this is contrary to anything I have ever known before. It looks strange but don't laugh. Phil makes it work incredibly. He is one of the most accurate chippers I have ever seen.

As I said, Galvano has some brand new theories. For instance, while actually stroking a putt, he says you should hold your breath to prevent body vibration. Have all your weight on the left foot—if it is equally divided your heartbeat will tend to make the body move. . . .

My friend John Mackie, of Hunstanton, used to say 'hold your putter as gently but securely as you would a baby's hand when you are teaching it to walk'. Galvano puts it another way. He says: 'Hold the putter as if it were a small bird. You wouldn't want it to fly away, nor would you wish to crush it.'

It is on the big golf strokes that Phil gets working on the medical aspect. He didn't actually ask me to strip naked for my lesson, but he did suggest that I should perform this way in front of a mirror at home. 'Watch the tension lines of your abdomen muscles,' he says. 'See that the ulva and radius bones of your arms are not crossed. It prevents sensitivity in the hands. . . .'

Try as I will it is almost impossible for me to depart for ever

"Now, you noticed the completion of my full pivot before allowing the easy recoil action to concentrate power of centrifugal force into the clubhead as the hands pronate after impact ...."

from the subject of putting. Galvano and most Americans now favour the Schenectady, or similar implements with the shaft joining the blade in the middle.

It's grand to know that even the pros say that in this department we can entirely please ourselves. A certain Mr. E. H. Taylor, who was a friend of Mr. Sydney Fry's and also a prominent member of the Royal Mid-Surrey Club, collected putters as some collect walking-sticks. They were his hobby and he bought new ones each Christmas and every time he had a birthday. In all, he had nearly two hundred, and these he kept in two adjoining lockers. John, the kindly steward, had permission to show them to any interested visitor.

The mention of Mr. Taylor gives me an opportunity to bring the memory of him forward as an example for you to follow unswervingly. Remember, E. H. was a very fine scratch golfer. Yet, it is on record that he once took ninety-six strokes to go round Mid-Surrey! His partner declares that not once did he use a swear word.

Yours,

DAD

P.S. I'm afraid this has become a long, long letter. Sorry. I can't sleep for thinking of Bill Corbett's expensive baby.

D EAR SON: 'Dearie, dearie me! What next?'—as
Mother used to say when I told her one of my cock-an'-bull
stories. I have just been hearing of an amazing Japanese golfer
who is alleged to make the ball go further from the tee than has
ever been done before. Rarely does he drive less than three
hundred and fifty yards.

The whole question of big hitting is fascinating. After all, that
was surely how the game of golf started. The business of knocking
the darned thing into little holes must have come long afterwards.
Probably because it is a department of the game in which I have
always suffered a deficiency, the mighty blow always commands
my profound respect. One or two demonstrations have left im-
prints on my memory which I am quite sure will be there until I
die. If there is anyone in the world whom I envy it is the man who
can drive a golf ball two hundred and fifty yards without the help
of downward slope or following wind.

There was the time I played with Cyril Tolley. No caddies, so
Tolley, who disdained mechanical contrivances, carried his clubs
(in a tatty old leather bag) over his shoulder like a musket.

First hole of our pleasant Hertfordshire course is 310 yards.
Tolley didn't even take his pipe from his mouth. What's more,
the club he used was of ancient vintage, loose string and all. I had
seen the first green driven before, but never so casually. It was
early springtime and I do not recall that the ground was hard,

39

neither did the wind blow noticeably. Yet Cyril's ball whee-ed through the air with a gentle drag, and finally died on the green.

The great Tolley was probably the longest driver of the 'twenties—amateur or professional—at a time when there were some mighty men around. In a long driving competition at Troon in 1925, he struck the ball 290 yards and 10 inches—a very considerable clout and well ahead of the other competitors on a day when conditions were not particularly favourable.

I have asked Cyril if he can name the secret of long hitting. He puts it into one word—'balance'. That gets me precisely nowhere and I have now almost decided that the downward slope of a mountain is the only answer so far as my golf is concerned.

The fifteenth hole at Royal Wimbledon measures 420 yards. From the tee you cross a ditch diagonally and the fairway rises gently until it is near the green which is quite high, in fact on a little plateau, on an elevation perhaps fifty feet above the level of the tee.

On a warm day in October 1929, a certain Mr. T. H. V. Haydon, who was then an advertising agent, smacked a ball which very nearly reached the green. The shot was testified by Mr. Tippett, the honest Secretary, who said the distance was 'about 400 yards'! Later, the exact distance was checked at 403 yards. So far as I can verify this is the longest non-fluke drive on record. Once or twice I have employed the caddie who was on the job that day. When we get to the fifteenth, somehow or other the conversation always gets round to the long hit. It is vastly entertaining to see the caddie bask in reflected glory. And I don't blame him.

Mr. Haydon left advertising to take over the lovely Branksome Towers Hotel, near Bournemouth. In his cosy bar I spoke to him about his big knock—in the meantime, twenty-eight years had passed. He said: 'Oh, yes, Royal Wimbledon. Nice course.' That was all. I had vaguely thought of tapping some deep memory in order to learn just how the goliath blow was struck. . . . But we had a gin, and Vernon Haydon talked of other things.

Distance achieved by a smitten golf ball is in direct relation to

clubhead speed at impact. Any mutt knows that. The difficult part is achieving clubhead speed.

Jolly Gene Sarazen, carrying out some tests in conjunction with an American automobile company, decided that the ball actually leaves his club at 130 miles an hour. The findings of this early experiment were revised in 1955, when photo-electric equipment tests showed the ball to be travelling at only 110.5 miles per hour at impact. In this case they used a mechanical striker. Perhaps Gene hit his ball harder.

Later, super-duper statistics on this subject are regularly issued by the Franklin Institute in Philadelphia. The eggheads use a 'pitchometer', which measures the speed of objects passing through photo-electric beams in its exterior. It has been proved that even the velocity of an arrow is many miles per hour slower than a sweetly struck golf ball. . . . Oh, well.

Possibly the most discussed of the mighty drives was the one which Henry Cotton launched from the twelfth tee at Walton Heath in 1938, when he and Whitcomb disputed £500 with Locke and Brews. The hole in question is a dog-leg to the right. Henry took the short cut, clearing rough country to land on the edge of the green. I doubt whether the same shot is possible today. The trees have grown.

I love Walton Heath—probably because it flatters my drives. Sandy soil and rolling country put a song into the heart of a well-struck golf ball and results are gratifying.

You will remember the fifteenth. Two hundred and seventy yards away there is a bunker which was once well-carried by Mr. Angus Hambro. He deserves this passing mention, particularly since this feat was performed long before you, my son, were born, and I think Mr. Hambro was playing with a gutty.

During most of the time James Braid was professional at Walton Heath he employed craftsman Bob Horsbrough, who has been described as 'the miracle clubmaker'. Bob recalls regular Tuesday afternoon foursomes, in which Lord Riddell and Mr. Hedley LeBas matched their prowess and wits against Mr. Lloyd George and James Braid.

'Great names,' says the craftsman, 'with no favours given or expected. Mr. Lloyd George would always take the drive at the eighteenth. He would trundle one up the middle, just clearing the gorsey ravine, and stopping on the brow of the hill. Then, Mr. Braid would take his brassie and crack one into the heart of the green 250 yards away. They always played the hole like that. . . .'

Big hitting is the shop-window of the golf game. I remember when Hogan, Snead, Bousfield, and Weetman stood on the first tee at Wentworth to drive off for the 1956 Canada Cup. Slammin' Sam and Hogan had reputations for hitting long 'uns. At that time Harry Weetman was the longest hitter of all the British professionals.

The atmosphere had a tang of expectancy that you could almost taste. Twenty thousand spectators wanted to see if Harry could out-smite the Americans. Snead had said—or the Press had said he'd said—he could 'see Weetman off' at long driving. Now we would know. It was a question of national pride.

'Never mind about your other seventeen drives, Harry, but please, oh please, give this one all you've got!' That's what our hearts were saying. As addicts, we deal in emotions, and our emotions called for Weetman to do his stuff at this very moment.

Hogan drove, long and straight. Then, Snead—A corker!—with enough draw on it to send the ground running away. Bousfield was straight, but thirty yards behind. Finally, beautiful, lovely, splendid Harry. . . . He started his pivot away down in his shoes, then lashed with all his might. The ball went on and on. . . .

Slammin' Sam was vanquished by at least ten feet. The crowd sighed with relief. Only the cads put into words what we all felt.

And now for the Jap whom I mentioned at the beginning of this letter. It appears that this quick-witted, muscular son of the orient has contrived a trick, whereby, in his lightning follow-through he actually *strikes the ball twice*! The speed is such that to the naked eye it appears as a single stroke.

Now, you can either take this, or toss it aside as fiddle-de-dee, but this extraordinary operation has been described to me by a man who regards golf much too sacredly for jest. Personally, I regard the phenomenon on a par with the Frank Reynolds' story of the chap who could make the flight of a golf ball write his initials!

Back to the Jap. We must now consider the following: The long-hitting oriental has just cracked one of his 'specials'. His opponent is undismayed, although he sees the Jap's ball finish 350 yards down the fairway. 'You're there for two, chum,' he says.

Yours,

DAD

"There was I, minding my own business, walking down by the golf course, when ...."

DEAR SON: This is one of those nights! They happen once in a while—more regularly, I fear, as the years pass —when one reflects on age and the sadness of it.

To the young, nothing seems more remote than a bald pate, a toothless cackle, and a golf shot played for safety. You, of course, being in the first rosy flush of lithesome youth, never think of these things. Why should you? The world is yours, and you can belt the ball a mile, without worrying whether or not you've torn out the staples of your guts.

The day will come, however, possibly when you are fortyish, when a passing thought will slip into your day. You will suddenly notice a chill in the air. Instead of clouting a great high parabola with a number seven for it to land on the green 'like a poached egg', you will gently pitch up to the pin with your mashie.

When this sad moment comes, and you realize with a shock that you are getting old, ere you become too depressed about it, please remember the name of Nathaniel Walter Vickers. This gentleman was unique. Although he died in 1949 his name will live so long as golf is remembered as the secret of longevity.

John Ellis Knowles, a senior American golfer of whom I have written in another place, knew Nathaniel Vickers and golfed with him on many occasions. Ellis is a good friend, also, he is a greatly respected member of the Royal and Ancient. With Francis Ouimet, and John Arthur Brown, of Pine Valley, he often crosses the

Now you litttle —

TEE THOUGHTS NO. 3

Atlantic for the express purpose of attending meetings at St. Andrews. To that extent he is a man of substance, so we have no reason to doubt what Ellis says about the quite amazing late Nathaniel Vickers.

Like my friend, Vickers was a prominent member of the United States Senior Golfers Association. In fact, he competed in all the Association competitions until he was ninety-six years old! On the day Mr. Vickers reached his century, he joined a party of friends for a day's golf. 'Sorry if this upsets your arrangements,' he said, 'but I only play nine holes consecutively. I play the other nine after lunch.'

This golfing paragon said his secret for living long, happily, was 'keeping an easy pace'. Either on the golf course, or in less important fields of activity, never change your steady gait. . . . Yet, Nathaniel Vickers was mentally agile, and practised as a successful architect. Although he lived most of his life in the United States, he was a Briton, from Moulton, in Lincolnshire.

I hope this comment on the age of a golf addict is reassuring. As I have so often advised, you should beg, borrow, or steal for yourself a smooth golf swing which will last for ever. Then the game will stick by you until the end, never letting you down, guarding the health, moulding character, and, more importantly, always comforting the troubled mind.

Is this morbid? Golf is never that. The game is rattling good fun. At least, that is the opinion of Mr. Sydney Harold Fry.

In 1902 Mr. Fry lost by one hole to Charles Hutchings in the final of the Amateur Championship. That was a long time ago, yet, fifty-six years afterwards, when I went forth this afternoon with my friend Dan Macfie to steer one with my driver on to the apron of the first green at Royal Mid-Surrey, 'Uncle Sydney' (as he is affectionately known) was going out with a handful of practise balls to 'try something new'. Mr. Fry, looking remarkably un-ruffled about it, had just celebrated his eighty-eighth birthday!

It is right that you should know about these splendid people.

The tenth Earl of Wemyss was before my time, but for colour and enthusiasm he must have been hard to beat. Golf was his life, as I hope it will be yours. He died in 1914 at the age of ninety-six, having played golf regularly from the age of fourteen until he was ninety-two. When he got weary of walking between shots, he rode sedately on the chestnut cob which always accompanied him. He was respected and admired in the whole Clyde countryside, a land where golf is rightly held in high regard.

Memories of these great figures from the past are usually dim

Between shots, the Earl of Wemyss rode sedately on a chestnut cob....

shadows, but there is still the brave James Sherlock, whom you have seen so often with our friend John Mackie on the lovely course at Hunstanton. Mr. Sherlock does not play often these days—he is worried with 'the screws'—but he would be a wealthy man if some philanthropist gave him just one sovereign for each round he has played at Hunstanton and Aldeburgh up to the time of this letter! He is eighty-three.

Mr. Sherlock has had a distinguished career, having played for England for six successive years at the beginning of the century. He held the record with 66 on the famous Le Touquet course, but the homely Norfolk links are his favourites, and on one of these he made fine history and gained a place in a short list of *élite*. At Aldeburgh, he holed-in-one, both the fourth and seventeenth during the same round.

James has had thirteen 'aces' and says he hopes to get off the unlucky number before his clubs are permanently passed on. . . .

That, my boy, is the stuff to give 'em.

You have had your hole-in-one, and that is something I envy. One flogs, and flogs, and hopes. Maybe I shall emulate Mr. Sydney Fry's old friend Mr. T. E. Lewis. At the age of seventy-eight he holed out at Mid-Surrey. The hole was 138 yards. He used a brassie. *Necessitas non habet legem.*

Yours,
DAD

" Don't tell me he's holed it !"

7

DEAR SON: In the mad, ruthless quest for the secret which makes one hit the ball further from the tee, I have just taken positive action. I hope my ruse will succeed, although past experience has taught me not to expect too much.

The reason why I acquired a new, rather special driver is not without interest.

In aeroplanes the question of weight is important. For this reason I have to admit, with some shame, that instead of taking fewer clothes in my trunk when I flew to the United States, I was persuaded to leave behind my golf clubs. This did not mean that my activities were to be curtailed. On the contrary, I had a heavy programme of play and looked forward to it all with enjoyable anticipation.

Before leaving London airport I was assured that wherever I went sets of golf clubs would be made available to suit my particular requirement. This, in fact, was the case. Only twice was I unlucky and I do not propose to go into details. Besides, on those occasions my hosts were so contrite that it would be churlish to mention the matter further.

At Evanston, near Chicago, Mike Kovansky produced for me a most unusual bag. It was bright red, with a shoulder strap fashioned from a strip of unshaved reindeer skin.

'These are my aunt's,' said Mike. 'She does okay with them —shoots in the seventies all the time.'

49

There were five woods, each wearing a fancy-tasseled cover. When I exposed the driver, to my delight I saw that the head had been enamelled pure white. The other woods were the same.

Mike explained: 'Auntie likes them that way. She says it helps her back swing. Even when she's looking hard at the teed up ball, from the corner of her eye she can see if the white clubhead is swinging smoothly back in the proper arc. . . .'

It made sense.

Anyway, granted that my normal standard is not high, with these unusual clubs I performed rather well. I beat my host and had the pleasure of hitting the ball better than usual. The putter was a mallet-type—foreign to my nature—so I used a two iron on the greens. In this department I enjoyed but small success. But the woods worked sweetly and I seemed to get run on the ball.

From time to time I have recalled the nice game at Evanston, and particularly my success with the 'albino' driver. Recently, having lost length from the tee at the rate of about a yard a week for months, I finally resolved to get Bob Kenyon, our Professional, to make me a driver to the following specifications. The shaft—short and whippy; the grip—good old-fashioned leather; the clubhead—heavy, and enamelled white.

I think the enamelling operation must have worried Bob, for when I took delivery the clubhead was not quite as ordered. It is, however, light-coloured, unstained persimmon, with such a beautiful finish that I simply hadn't the heart to ask for a coat of white paint.

With this useful club I am now persevering. So far, the results don't come up to my Evanston round, but once in a while, for no apparent reason, I hit a long one and this gives me encouragement and hope for the future. I have seen Bob hit scorchers with this weapon, and of course when I let my friends handle it they all say, 'Hm, there's nothing wrong with the *club*. . . .'

One never despairs. Every golf addict has a little reserve of something or other in the locker, and I don't mind admitting that if I am not striking the ball really well with this Kenyon club by the time the lovely polish has dimmed, I shall secretly dip the head until it is pure as driven snow. I am convinced that my extra yardage may well be found in a tin of white enamel.

Writing thus of my equipment problems has set me thinking of yours. Days pass. Your homecoming to golf excitingly approaches, and I can imagine your nostrils distended like a bloodhound's scenting the kill. Already your feet tingle at the thought of springy fairways. You sense the joyful message in your fingers, surging through to your vitals . . . as a long one cracks off the driver like a bullet.

It is quite certain that you are considering your first major financial outlay. I mean, for a new set of irons.

Cyril Tolley once declared that in his opinion the steel tube manufacturer, having edged the golf club craftsman out of business, is now in the process of making life very difficult for all

1 Hands high, split-second pause,

2 —then pull down with the left, keeping right elbow in.

3 Don't uncock until hands are level with your hips . . .

4 Don't quit with your left . . keep the arm straight

professionals who cannot make a good income from tournaments. When steel shafts were first introduced, the professionals should have seen the red light and scotched the idea at birth. As things are going, it is quite possible that sets of these heartless, standardized clubs may one day even be on sale in tobacconists' shops!

These efficient shiny things do perform beautifully, but the good old friendly bespoke golf clubs, affectionate and personal, are greatly missed. Before you have made your decision to buy, let me sketch in for you my experience of golf equipment.

We start with the seven clubs my friend Bert Ashby made for me nearly thirty years ago. In a secondhand leather bag (which crumpled a bit, but looked very 'senior') I carried a driver-brassie, a spoon, a mid-iron, a jigger, a mashie, a niblick, and a putter. The latter has been in use until recently and stands

5 Still holding on with the left, lash through with the right —

6 taking care not to raise your head until the ball is away

7 and your body swings through ... relaxed

in my umbrella-stand as an efficient reserve should the occasion demand.

These clubs served me well until the last war. Then, on return from the disturbance, I bought for what seemed a colossal amount of money a matched set of American Eagle irons, neatly numbered two to nine. To these I added three very respectable woods, each protected by a leather bonnet. The old putter remained, isolated perhaps, but the only thing in the bag for which I had any real attachment.

Hacking, sclaffing, foozling, occasionally doing the right thing . . . these weapons lasted me for two or three years. My golf was a little worse than before the war, but that was natural with the appearance of grey hair. Then, as the weather in some extraordinary way each year seemed to deteriorate, one had the need to carry an umbrella and waterproofs. Caddie cars, instead of being novelties became a recognized part of the golfing scene. Our professional Bert Ashby sent for some, and I bought one.

At about this time folk seemed to talk more about special high-velocity golf balls, plastic tees, wedges, left-handed gloves, and so on. It was all very interesting and perhaps the extra expense was worth the fun and the forlorn hope that maybe one's game would improve. But when some lunatic experimented with the grips on golf clubs it rather got my goat. Before the war golf club grips were always leather strips, skilfully wound, rasped when shiny, and anointed with castor oil to keep them tacky. Following the craze for gimmicks, all-weather, non-slip, rubber grips started to be popular. Then they started making them of compounds of rubber and cork, rubber and canvas, corrugated rubber, and so on.

Of course, like my friends, I fell for the lot. Why shouldn't I benefit like others who were now finding the game so easy? (That is the sort of conversation I have been having with myself ever since I started the game!)

Off to the Pro's shop I went to arrange new grips for my set. But I never put the order in hand. As an outcome of a pleasant chat I became the owner, not only of a brand new set of Bobby Locke Gradidge irons, but also a new set of four Bobby Locke woods.

54

Wind with me — watch me scuffle it ! ....

Having spent about £60 on this lot it seemed ridiculous not to invest another couple of pounds on a new style set of leather covers for the woods.

If the occasion ever arises when you are called upon to strap an old-fashioned leather golf bag on to a modern, sorbo-tyred caddie car (that was my next investment) you will find that it simply won't work. You need a non-crumpling club container, built with huge udders to carry shoes, clothing, towels, and what have you. Some go in for up-to-date, rain-resisting, plastic bags, but I am allergic to plastics, so decided to have one specially made. It is fabricated of tough canvas-silk, and reinforced with leather, with a special strong inlay where there is friction from the caddie-car.

With this carefully chosen equipment I have mostly enjoyed my golf during the past four years. I play on many courses all over the country and admit that when travelling by train, or staying in good hotels, people eye my bag with considerable respect. True that after thirty-six holes my caddies usually wilt and I have to give extra payment as compensation, but still . . . Without doubt there are certain advantages to owning a mammoth set of golfing paraphernalia, but at the moment I cannot think of them.

The time now approaches when you must give consideration to these questions. It is my belief that a similar range of equipment to that which I have described will be your choice. If so, you must expect to spend about £100.

This is severe, but if you go the whole hog, I shall not blame you. Spending cash on golf clubs and all the oddments they say we need is the normal routine in the development of every golf addict.

Do not imagine, however, that it ends when you are all fixed up with the best of everything. One is never satisfied. Golf, like art, must be progressive. . . .

At this moment I am considering an important streamlining operation. I am thinking of selling my stuff, and buying a small canvas bag in which I can carry seven clubs—a driver-brassie, a spoon, a mid-iron, a jigger, a mashie, a niblick, and my old putter.

Yours,

DAD

"Seven? — sure you didn't take eight?"

8

DEAR SON: Having just enjoyed my favourite dream—doing a hole-in-one—I now awaken, remembering that it is a while since I wrote to you. Here goes.

Few games offer a player the possibility of perfection. Golf does. Perfection? Yes, but that is describing a hole-in-one in a bloodless, cold way. You remember how an insensitive doctor once described love's high spot? 'A human kiss,' he said, 'is the contact and gentle pressure of lips when they are made to touch.' Dreadful.

As with a passion-loaded kiss, I doubt whether words could ever adequately describe an 'ace' at golf. I mean, so far as the emotions are concerned. I have played the game for thirty years, yet never have I experienced the divine thrill of a hole-in-one. I am, therefore, ill-qualified to attempt a description of how a golfer feels at the sublime moment.

However, having accompanied my friend Ted Long when he celebrated a Whit Monday that way, and also having once played with a man named Desmond Sprockett, whose topped spoon shot made the ball shoot along the ground, hit a hillock, leap violently over a bunker, land on the green, and finally roll into the hole. . . . I may be permitted to touch on a subject which really merits a wiser pen than mine.

Golf's supreme accomplishment can having devastating effects. This man Sprockett became glassy-eyed. We had three holes still to play, yet he insisted on walking in because he mustn't have his bliss disturbed! He was in seventh heaven and intended to stay like that as long as possible. The peak of his high mountain was reached and he must linger to enjoy the view.

One of the nicest holes-in-one came to my young friend Howard Fagan. As a twenty-first birthday present to himself he aced the fifteenth at Leatherhead.

He was playing in an Open Medal Competition. Howard didn't win the contest but his effort at the fifteenth will long be talked in the bar. Slight dog-leg, uphill; distance 270 yards. His father said, 'I would like to be able to hit a ball as far!' That also goes for me. Of course Howard was elated (who wouldn't be?). So was the President of the Club. He dashed off and bought a beautiful silver cigarette casket. It was waiting for young Fagan when he got in.

Now, son, in your relatively short golfing career you have had a hole-in-one. That ball which you perched up on the second tee at Letchworth had a destined fate long before you struck it with a golf club. Within the rubber core there was magic, and what happened had to happen, with practically no effort from you.

In all the golf holes which I have enjoyed (or endured) not once has there been magic within my ball. Not on the tee, at any rate. Yet, more than once I have addressed a ten-foot putt and felt completely certain that the ball when struck would roll smoothly to the hole and drop. On those lovely but rare occasions it always does. I clearly feel the magic, not only in my hands, but coursing through all my veins.

You will say this is merely a question of confidence. Call it what you like, but I suggest that no one can honestly claim that while on the tee they have ever felt *absolutely certain* that their drive will finish in the hole. No. One never 'feels' that the drive will finish in the hole. One 'hopes', and that is why I say that the ball takes matters into its own hands, for aces.

The striker's part in the operation, although necessary, is small. If you want proof, here it is. Alex Herd is on record as having done nineteen aces. James Braid did eighteen, yet Harry Vardon (possibly the greatest golfer the world has known) is only on record as having done the trick once!

Putting Point

Don't 'sight' outside the ball

Check the length of your putter—

Your eye should be <u>exactly</u> <u>over</u> <u>the ball</u>

you mustn't stoop too much

Either the ball is, or isn't, possessed of magic. The player is not always told about it.

Yet I have a case in mind which contradicts this theory. A scratch golfer stood on the eighteenth tee of a 460 yards bogey five hole. For the seventeen holes, he had played a total of seventy shots. Par for the course was seventy-two. He had taken a bet with long odds that he would go round to his handicap, or better. That is to say, taking no more than seventy-two strokes.

Standing on the tee of this long last hole he knew that only an albatross could win for him a substantial sum of money. He had a good drive. For his second shot—about 220 yards—he took a brassie. 'This is going in the hole,' said the player, dead serious.

There were a dozen or so spectators. No one spoke. What was there to say? It was the sort of comment one often makes to kid oneself into confidence.

The golfer looked around. 'This is going in the hole,' he repeated.

And it did.

Afterwards, the player told friends that while addressing the ball he had a *positive feeling* that it would finish in the cup!

A saga could be written on this fascinating aspect of golf. I only hope that the day will come when I may write with the authority of practical experience. According to my reckoning: approximately 200 rounds a year (each round with three short holes), for twenty-five years (allowing for war interference) the odds against me getting an ace must be at least 15,000 to 1.

An American professional named Harry Gouder once decided that he would keep hitting balls until he got an ace. The hole was 160 yards. With caddies and witnesses he cracked away for sixteen hours twenty-five minutes. After 941 tee shots he stopped for food. His 996th hit the pin and stopped three inches away. His 1,756th refused when it had only one inch to go. After 1,817 shots it was getting dark and Harry could hardly see. He said 'to hell with it' and vowed never even to think of holing-in-one again.

When I played at the Army and Navy Country Club, at

Washington, I met a young assistant professional named Ted McClandish. This is his story.

A prominent member of the Washington Country Club, who manufactured boots and shoes, made a habit of giving a pair to everyone at his Club who had a hole-in-one. He was playing ahead of Ted when the performance took place. Ted did an ace and one of his companions shouted over to the shoe-man that a pair of shoes had been earned. The shoe-man replied that Ted, being a professional, would only get one shoe instead of a pair. Believe it or not, but a hole later, young McClandish actually repeated the performance! I understand that Ted's feat gained for him an even greater reward. He need never pay for another pair of shoes as long as he lives.

It is rather nice to know that instead of the feat costing you cash, under certain circumstances, there is a reward. At the Royal Ashdown Forest Club, in Sussex, the Island Hole is a gem. A Mr. Lionel Redpath has endowed it for £5 and the accumulated interest goes to whomsoever has the good fortune to ace it on certain competition days. This happened many years ago and the last news I had was that no one so far has succeeded, although the interest grows.

For holes-in-one, golf balls must carry magic. Neither the player nor the venue matters. For instance, a man named Mr. F. C. Sidney was practising driving the 120 yard sixth at the Isle of Scilly Golf Club. He played three balls from the tee. The green is saucer-shaped and the view from the tee is partly obscured by a stone wall. On reaching the green Mr. Sidney found two of his balls in the hole and the other, which could well have hit the flag, was only a few inches away!

Aces always produce excitement. I remember when a team of us crossed the Channel to play Rouen my pal Jimmy Randle did a hole-in-one on the pleasant course at Mont St. Aignan. The French were jubilant, so was Jimmy, but he kept a stiff upper lip to let our hosts see that this was nothing really exceptional for a Briton to do!

Really great events have happened north of the border. Jock

Keep your big fat head down ...

Hutchison had a hole-in-one at St. Andrews when he won the Open in 1921. I have seen the mashie that did the trick. It is on display in the Golf Museum at New York and a card tells that the same weapon was used on fifteen similar occasions, although the shaft had been changed three times. . . .

Holes-in-one must have been giving their own particular brand of thrills for centuries. Yet, the first recorded case was as recently as 1868 when young Tom Morris aced the eighth at Prestwick in an Open tournament. I have been unable to ascertain the facts of this memorable event. Possibly young Tom made one of his dour comments, but I am quite sure that within his Scottish breast there was the same surge of red hot emotion which you yourself experienced on the second at Letchworth.

Another Scot, my friend McEwan King, told me of a hole-in-one he witnessed at Aboyne.

Aboyne is the perfect course for a hole-in-one. There are hardly ever any members there during the week, and the club-house is unlicensed anyway.

Mac was touring the Scottish courses with George Scott, of Hilton Park. On the seventeenth at Aboyne, George played with a wedge from the tee. According to Mac, the ball was hooked a bit to the left of the green. Instead, in fairness, of finishing in a sand trap, the ball kicked violently into the air, hit the cloth of the flag and dropped plonk! into the hole. George howled with delight.

A groundsman appeared from nowhere carrying two quart beer bottles. 'Did ye jist get an ace, sir?' asked the old Scot.

'I did that,' said George.

'Then, sir,' said the groundsman, 'I reckon you deserve a drink.'

'Thanks,' said George, grabbed one of the beer bottles, and took a long swig. Unfortunately the bottle contained oil for the gang mower!

One of the saddest stories I know was enacted at Hunstanton.

One sunny morn', a kindly old chap had the thrill of hitting a sweet one at the short over-the-hill hole. He discovered his ball in the cup.

Back at the clubhouse he did the honours proudly. To the fifty or so golfers in the bar and public rooms he declared this to be the happiest day of his life. For nearly sixty years he had played golf, had almost despaired of ever attaining the 'perfection shot'. Then, on this lovely day, almost at the end of his golfing career, the miracle had occurred. The old boy's eyes filled with tears of pure joy. Then some damned fool non-golfing woman, sitting out on the verandah, mentioned that her wretched brat of a son saw the ball come bouncing over the hill. He put it in the hole—for fun!

Yours,

DAD

9

DEAR SON: As you know, disbelievers constantly attack me for spreading golf. In fact, Mother says that her only anxiety for your future is your hereditary love for the game—for which she blames me.

Never mind. During your absence I shall continue these regular golf injections and I hope they will keep your appetite whetted for that first great game which we shall enjoy together within minutes of your return to England.

As soon as I get your telegram I shall have things lined up. If your ship arrives at Liverpool, the magnificent course at Hoylake it will be. If you berth at Southampton, we shall have our game at Stoneham. As a third alternative we know that quite close to the Heath Row airport is pleasant Stoke Poges, and that may well be where we ultimately play our first game. The Eton Rural District Council, which has just taken over the club, will have much to answer for if things go wrong.

But all that is for the future. My thoughts tonight, for some reason which I cannot understand, are of women.

I mean women golfers.

Some are not out of place in the golfing scene. Nevertheless, set against the nagging millions of unsympathetic wives (they call themselves 'golf widows', and expect everyone to cry!) I doubt whether the final balance would decide that women golfers have given enough to the game to compensate for their disagreeable sisters.

"What do I do next?"

They have caused a deal of unrest.

As a matter of fact, it could truthfully be said that women players have done little more than add a mere seasoning of mildly funny stories to the annals of golf.

'I don't care for mixed-foursomes,' says a female to her girl-friend. '—The men only talk about *golf*.'

That sort of thing.

Yet, even were we empowered, I doubt whether more than one male golfer in five would wish to ban women from every course in the country. Most of us are tolerant folk, merely aggravated by incidents and circumstance.

Cross my heart, the following is true. It will infuriate you.

An elderly woman, white-haired and infirm on her feet, was having tea beneath that nice shady tree by the putting-green at the Royal Wimbledon Golf Club. Her son, who was putting, called her over. 'Have a go,' he said. The old lady, not very amused, took the putter. She held it with her hands about eight inches apart and the nose of the putter head pointing to the sky. Then she sloshed at a ball. Straight as a die it careered towards the little flag fifteen yards away and dropped into the hole!

The old lady turned away. 'I don't know what all the fuss is about,' she said. Having performed her solitary golf shot with complete perfection, she sat down again under the shady tree and resumed tea.

Her golf addict son expostulated and tried to explain that it wasn't really as easy as that, but the old lady waved him away, refusing the suggestion that she should just try to do it again. . . . Having listened to her son and his foolish friend discuss every single shot they had made during their afternoon round, she did not intend to suffer further boredom with either the theories or practice of a stupidly simple game.

"—And don't tell me that's not inspired!"

The old lady took her knitting, and only occasionally glanced up at the two young men who seemed to find it so extraordinarily difficult to hit their little balls into the holes on the lawn.

Now, will you tell me how one could possibly cope with such a situation? The son, whom I know well, had my deepest sympathy. Try until he is blue in the face, he will never persuade his mother that golf is actually much more difficult than it looks.

You have heard me mention the name of Mrs. George Valentine. As wee Jessie Anderson she used to hit the ball like a master on the North Inch, at Perth, even when she was a little girl. For upwards of fifty years her father Joe has been the professional at the Craigie Club. Jessie and I used to play together—not golf, but hopscotch, and other kiddie games—while our respective fathers went off to a Perthshire rifle range. Joe Anderson, a small man, would be correctly described as an all-rounder. Not only has he played golf many times for Scotland but also is an international cricketer and curler. It was natural that wee Jessie should attain the heights.

All this just to say that Mrs. Valentine is strictly on the credit side of women's golf. So is Lady Amory (Miss Joyce Wethered) who played eight times for her country; Miss Cecilia Leitch, twelve times international; and, of course, the astonishing Babe Zaharias, who not only established herself for a brief spell as the finest woman golfer in the world, but also actually won three gold medals at the Olympic Games.

But, in my opinion, Jessie is the greatest of them all. To the time of writing she has played for Scotland no fewer than fifty-eight times!

These are 'female greats' who come to mind. It is a pity that there is another side of the picture. The following appeared in the *Daily Mirror* newspaper.

Ever since my husband started playing golf two years ago our household has ceased to be normal. He's up early every morning to try to get a few holes in before he leaves for work, and he's out with his golfing pals as soon as he gets a free moment. The home is

"My wife prefers to play with my best friend — whoever he is..."

littered with clubs, balls, and books on the game, and now he's threatened to move to a house nearer a golf course.

The letter was signed by a lady from Woodford, Essex.

In a divorce action, Mr. Justice Willmer said, 'If a woman marries a golf addict that is one of the things that come within the phrase "For better or for worse".' That makes the position clear, but I would like to see *Mr.* Woodford in my consulting room. Without in any way restricting his golfing activities—which can be regarded as normal—I think there are certain things which can be done to harmonize the domestic side of his life.

First of all, he could invite his wife to go with him to golf. Encourage her to take an interest. She could pull his caddie-car. Then, Mr. Woodford might well solicit the help of a golfing friend of mine, the astonishing Mrs. Florence Macaulay. She knows all about the game from a woman's point of view. I would gamble that at the end of half an hour of conversation Mrs. Woodford of Essex would be out playing herself!

Mrs. Macaulay lives near Birmingham. She plays golf every day of her life either at Edgbaston, Robin Hood, or Moor Hall. She is an honorary member of all three. Her handicap is now twelve, but once it was three. She is eighty-six years old.

I asked this marvellous lady why she did not start golf until late in life. She gave me this horrifying answer. 'Until I was forty-five I was much too busy playing tennis!'

The strongest part of Mrs. Macaulay's game is her approaching and putting, and in this she falls into line with all those other wonderful folk who have designed and fabricated a golf swing to last a lifetime. The mechanism never changes.

At the beginning of this letter I belittled the contribution which women have made to golf. As usual, I was prejudiced by emotions which always overcome me when I think of non-golfing wives bullying addicted hubbies. Let no one say that Florence Macaulay is not an asset to the game. For years she has crusaded and cajoled towards happier golfdom. Have you heard of the Warwickshire Veteran Ladies' Association? Founded by Mrs. Macaulay, it has an enthusiastically robust membership. To be eligible, ladies must be over fifty years old. Keen? There isn't one of them whose hubby won't have to massage her back muscles before the Autumn Meeting!

Yours,
DAD

"Did you notice that frightful old jumper Angela's wearing?"

DEAR SON: In the railway compartment, on my way to the office this morning, the conversation turned to ancient Rome, the monuments, amphitheatres, and relics which this venerable civilization has left scattered over Europe and North Africa.... Someone mentioned Carthage, Cirene and Pompeii, all of which I know. Then a chap said that our own St. Albans is as interesting as many places further afield. Here was the opportunity for which I had waited with some impatience. I grabbed the conversation.

'Ah, Ancient Verulam,' I sighed. Then, before the compartment could stop me, I had slipped in a bit about the pleasant (but sometimes muddy) Verulam golf course which has one of the longest eighteenth holes on any British terrain.

This severe drag at the end of a heavy round usually separates the men from the boys. It is not a very good golf hole, but it promotes an excellent thirst which can be quenched in a jolly clubhouse. Past Captain Jack Kellard will be there. He makes a point of entertaining all casual visitors, and his cheery welcome is one of the things which makes golf something apart....

Along these lines, I tried to interest the regulars in our compartment. But it is not easy, and at the mention of golf they all raised their newspapers either to hide savage mutterings, or to do the crossword puzzles.

I wanted to take the talk from the eighteenth at Verulam to

HANDICAP GALLERY

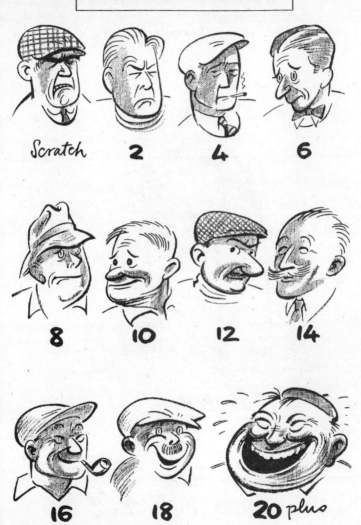

Scratch 2 4 6

8 10 12 14

16 18 20 plus

other long holes, such as the sixth at Troon. Then, I would have skipped lightly over to the United States and capped the conversation by telling the compartment about two real giants. Both the Coharrick Country Club in New Jersey, and a course at Hot Springs have holes measuring more than 700 yards.

"Think of the fun I got from that one!"

The only one of my companions who did not stay buried in newsprint surfaced only to show me how a new slide-rule could answer almost any question you were likely to ask.

I was far away. The word Verulam had prompted memories of a hundred golfing oddities. Did you hear of the golfer—reported in a newspaper despatch from Sydney—who followed his drive into the rough and stumbled upon a tin containing £240 worth of gold dust! This happened on the Peak Hill course, near Parkes, which in 1880 was the scene of the great New South Wales Gold Rush. You would have thought that even the non-golfers in our compartment would have been interested in that. Not on your life.

The other day I tried this on them. An Irish golfer sliced his ball into one of the Killarney Lakes and knocked out a trout which happened to be rising to catch a fly. The compartment howled me down.

I get so impatient with folk who cannot accept the unusual. Anyone who keeps his eyes and ears open must believe in fairies, and golf miracles.

Don't you like the story of Mrs. Francis White, J.P.? She performed the inaugural drive-off ceremony when a new course was opened near Manchester. It was very sporting of her to accept, having never touched a golf club in her life before.

There was to be a tournament between two well-known players, but before the start the Club Captain addressed the crowd from the first tee, introduced Mrs. White and announced that to her would go the first honour. Then, he teed up a golf ball nice and high, and handed a club to the distinguished lady guest, for her to hit the ball which would declare the course open for play.

Poor soul, knowing nothing about it, I suppose she giggled a bit, held the club like an axe, and asked which hand should go above which. Then she took a whack. Believe it or not the ball went so far and straight that the first player in the tournament gallantly enquired if he could take Mrs. White's shot for his drive!

That is what I like about golf. It encourages folk to say the nicest things. Some folk.

"Now there's a coincidence! — you had a four at the fifth and I had a nine at the tenth!"

I am always sorry for those who have the misfortune to live humdrum lives. One need not be a travelled adventurer to have the thrills. Take, for instance, my golfing friend Waterhouse to whom the most extraordinary things happen. He recounts them with great charm.

We played together yesterday, both put up a pitiful performance, yet seldom have I had more enjoyment from a game of golf. It happened to be the qualifying round of the *Evening News* Competition. Early in the round we both slipped in a couple of consecutive sixes, wrongly decided we hadn't a hope, so settled down to leisurely golf—with talk.

Waterhouse learnt his golf in an unusual way. He was a young subaltern gunner at Sheerness, occupied with coastal defences in the First World War. One of his brother officers was a plus-two golfer who knew what the game was all about. So he took my friend to golf. Being beneath sea-level the course at Sheerness is crisscrossed with waterways. The first lesson was with 'floaters'—balls which don't submerge in the dykes, a fact which hasn't hindered Waterhouse from becoming a first-class senior golfer.

Everything happens to Waterhouse. Once, while stopping at an inn called 'The Why-Not', on the Rugby road, he stood a drink to

"We're still digging a little..."

Now, be nice to me sweetheart ....

an old country yokel. There followed the usual routine, with a difference.

'Do 'ee play darts?' asked the old 'un. Waterhouse knew nothing about the game but said he'd try. He was politely handed three old 'feathers'. Wondering if he could make them stick in, my pal tossed one towards the board. A bullseye! The old 'un made appropriate comment, and said, 'Now 'ee get a double twenty.' Waterhouse did just that. By this time, the landlord and others in the saloon were taking a lively interest.

'What do I do now?' asked my friend. The old 'un roared. 'Ho, ho, what does the gen'man do now? Why, he gets a treble, o' course.'

Waterhouse did get a treble. And that was that. Wise enough not to go near the board again, my friend finished off his drink and left.

When he was a soldier, Waterhouse was convalescent in the Uppingham Workhouse. He used to walk alongside the field watching boys of the famous school playing rugby football. My friend attended a soccer school and I think he performed reasonably well. He is a powerful chap, so I would expect him to have a hefty kick, but excepting for this one occasion which I shall describe, Waterhouse never in his life attempted to kick an oval ball.

He had been watching two or three Uppingham chaps punting a rugger ball about and practising kicking goals. One of them invited him to have a go. Waterhouse balanced the ball carefully on the centre line and kicked it hard. Helped by a fair wind the ball sailed far and true right between the goalposts!

I have transgressed from golf but I wanted to tell you of Waterhouse. Now you shall learn of a passage of pure poetry that touched his life years ago while he was surf-riding at Newquay in Cornwall.

Big Atlantic breakers were making excellent sport and more than once Waterhouse had skimmed shorewards at great and exhilarating speed. Board under his arm, he was trudging out again to repeat the fun, when a surf-rider came rushing straight at him. It was an anxious moment, particularly for my friend. This breath-taking split second—just long enough for reflexes to take evasive action—was filled with a great roar from the man on the board. 'FORE!' he shouted, and streaked past, leaving my friend pleasantly aghast.

Waterhouse never saw him again. The unknown surf-rider was lost in foam.

No doubt both characters went on living their separate lives. But my friend, at any rate, would have liked them to have met. The man's cry of warning, unpremeditated, straight from the heart of his subconscious, was a music usually heard in green places where lasting friendships are made. . . .

Now I shall strike a discordant note.

A man I know who wastes his time playing squash copied out on a piece of paper the following. I understand it was originally written in jest by John D. Sheridan in a book sub-titled 'The Intelligent Rabbit's Guide to Golf'. I showed the document to my friends in the compartment of our railway train. As you may imagine it caused hilarity, which made me feel quite sick. Men whom I describe as friends take the same serious view as I do,

79

"Might I suggest you cure that slice — until income tax deductions are agreed for lost balls!"

particularly since we learn that other copies of the scandalous sheet have been anonymously sent through the post.

The work of a gang is suspected. Someone is trying to alienate our affections. The fact that there is basic truth in the message shows how diabolically clever are these under-cover destroyers.

Please burn this when read. We must not allow the poison to spread.

The John Sheridan piece reads:

Any pleasure there is in golf comes from hitting the ball, but as soon as you begin to hit it regularly and with skill you come up against the astounding contradiction that the whole aim is to hit the ball as seldom as possible. The better you play, the less you play: The more you play the worse you are. In fact, as golf gets better it tends to eliminate itself!

Smart stuff. But how dangerous! Evil influences moving among men are attempting to storm the Royal and Ancient citadel. Subversive propagandists spread moth-eaten tags like 'Golf—a good walk spoilt', etc., hoping to make us turn our clubs into fishing rods, or even carpet beaters.

We should not take this lying down. Attack! must be our battle cry. Tomorrow I shall have my secretary turning the handle of a duplicator until sparks fly. We will produce our own pamphlet to

scatter from helicopters over the crowds at Wimbledon, the Oval, and the Boat Race. Maybe we shall also take in Twickenham and the Arsenal Football ground.

How is this for text? The tract was written by the late Earl Balfour in 1884, when he won the Parliamentary Golf Tournament.

The wit of man has never invented a pastime equal to golf for its healthful recreation, its pleasurable excitement, and its never ending source of amusement.

Is it any wonder Balfour became Prime Minister?

Yours,

DAD

11

DEAR SON: We do not often speak of your future. Maybe I have under-emphasized the importance of grooving a durable golf swing, and establishing a design for living which will bring health, wealth, and happiness. The latter usually follows the first two—but also you must have a sweet golf swing.

Today, I have lunched with a friend whom I would classify high in the hierarchy of golf addicts. Like ourselves, he lives for the game. He has accepted a wonderful new appointment which I think you will agree is the final stroke in a design for living which can hardly be improved. The career of Graeme Nicholl could serve as a blueprint for our kind of folk who are prepared to toss something back into the game which has given us more than we can adequately repay.

Fifty-eight years old, at the conclusion of a long and distinguished business career in the Far East, Graeme now undertakes the secretaryship of the swankiest, idyllic golf club in the world—the Mid-Ocean, Bermuda. I once had a month there, and although a quarter of a century has passed, I can still glow at the thought of the place.

All addicts have had the dream at one time or another. Golf, under the nicest possible circumstances, in the sunshine. . . . All day, and every day. Not simply *playing* golf, but talking it, thinking it, living it. . . . As a job!

Of course he will have administrative work and all the *petites*

embêtements which go with Golf Clubs. Nevertheless, to a large extent Graeme will be controlling the best of all games, played on smooth terrain laid out on a lovely coral reef in the azure Caribbean. The life of Graeme Nicholl—as yet in his prime—will be sun-kissed for years to come. Strength to his elbow, and if I am mighty envious, I bear no ill-will. Some day, I shall get on one of those lovely ships at Southampton, or La Rochelle, and sail westwards to see how he is getting on.

The last time I played at Mid-Ocean was in 1933. One or two things I remember vividly: the pleasant 'over the sea' fifth hole, the rows and rows of millionaires' names on the little brass plates in the locker-room; a long table with an amazing variety of 'cold cuts' in the restaurant (this was a feature then), and the cheeriest negro caddies you could ever meet. . . .

The clubhouse is a Country Club with de luxe amenities, and although my personal taste leans more towards the simplicity of Royal Mid-Surrey, there is also much to be said for lush comfort.

Nicholl is just the man for the job. His main duty is to 'get folk —preferably the wealthy—interested in Bermuda golf'. He will jolly things up and popularize this golfing mecca. Although there is nothing in the world less like gowf at Saint Andrews, addicts will go to Mid-Ocean in their droves and find it good.

Graeme Nicholl has thousands of golfing friends, more than anyone I know, and this could only apply to a man who is saturated in the game. To begin with, Graeme is a cracking good player. His handicap (and he plays to it) is five. But like Bob Allen, another of my addict friends, although Graeme loves to play well, he would sooner play bad golf than no golf at all. Like many of us, he likes to talk golf and honestly believes that it is the one thing in life that can't be talked out.

At our meeting today we chattered for three solid hours, yet neither of us (and each had his turn) said one sentence which did not have a direct bearing on golf! Then we went up to Graeme's room at the Junior Carlton Club and practised swinging a brassie until the bangs on the floor got dangerously frequent. When we

85

parted, we both felt that time had rushed and that there was lots more to say.

Until the start of his new life, Graeme played most of his golf on the Royal Singapore course where the rainfall would stagger us in Britain. A hundred inches a year is commonplace, but it soon goes and play is seldom stopped for long.

From this base Graeme toured the world, playing everywhere, Bel Air—California, St. Andrews (he is a member of the R. and A., Woking, Littlestone), Burning Tree, Sunningdale, Pine Valley. . . . Hundreds of courses, in all the countries of the world. . . . At the Hungjao Club in Shanghai, he once played in an exhibition four-ball with Hagen and Kirkwood.

He plays with the Lucifers, the association of golfers from afar. In 1936, when amateur Bobby Locke won their competition, Graeme was third. He is usually among the pots.

Once, at Royal Singapore, Graeme returned a magnificent seventy-six. He collected a big silver cup, a handsome sweep, and many congratulations. Then he went to the locker-room to

The man who put the
<u>sun</u> in Sunningdale

change. His Chinese caddie, shaking with terror, was waiting at the door. Poor Graeme learnt that a number four iron, which he had been trying out on the previous day, had accidentally been left in his bag—*making fifteen clubs*! Graeme rushed back to the scene of the prize distribution and explained that by accident his golf bag had contained more than the permissible number of clubs. He was disqualified. They took away his fine silver cup, but later gave him another. It is very small, and in the bottom there is a hole with the engraved message 'Pull your finger out!'

In another letter I shall tell you of Graeme's hero. He toils in a shrine above New York's Fifth Avenue and his name is Ernest Jones. In Graeme's opinion, Jones is the greatest golf instructor of all times. Each word the maestro murmurs Graeme retains as a pearl of wisdom.

Before leaving Singapore he received a letter from Ernest Jones. I have permission to send you this extract:

It is such a shame that the word 'swing' has been so loosely used and the effects produced by the camera have been so grossly exaggerated that the word has lost its real meaning. Golf has been played for hundreds of years and if any tip was good, it would have become common knowledge long before now. As I see it, all this time has been devoted to looking for the latest tip to improve the swing, instead of understanding what the swing actually is, and developing it by practice, patience and perseverance. We humans are trying to buy skill. Knowledge is acquired by seeking, but wisdom is acquired by experience, and the experience of one will never convince another. However, we must live in hope and hope for the best.

Those are the words of an astonishing man. He must wait for my next letter.

Yours,
DAD

DEAR SON: Already I have told you of the lovable old professional who first fastened my diapers, coaxed me gently, scolded heartily, and finally got me on terms of such friendliness with golf that the game has gobbled up my life.

It happened years ago, but I remember my mentor explaining to me all about the implements we use. 'Now, young man,' he said, 'the shaft of a golf club could be made of hoak, or helm. . . . On the other 'and, it could be hash. As a matter of fact it's neither. It's 'ickory.'

Ernest Jones is also one of the old school. But he is one of the new school too, and it has been reasonably assessed that he has attained more successes (in cash and results) than any other golf tutor.

Jones gives something like three thousand lessons a year.

The National Golf Foundation of the U.S.A. states that in North America eighty-one million golf rounds are played annually. Ernest Jones has motivated a good many of them.

Directly or indirectly, golf has earned a million dollars for this great teacher. He is a man of substance with a lovely home on Long Island, and an academy on the seventh floor of a fine building among rich jewellers, couturiers, and swank shops on Fifth Avenue.

Mr. Jones attends his business each morning in a smart navy blue suit and he always has a home-grown rose in his buttonhole.

The Fifth Avenue golf academy has been compared to a doctor's surgery. Not that it is fitted up that way. In fact, the room is simple, which is okay since it must always be the scene of great humility.

I took in the Jones Golf School on the day I visited the United Nations building, three Manhattan churches, and the driving range at Forest Hills. Ernest wasn't there but three pupils were awaiting his return. I chatted with them and heard something of the 'how to learn golf' technique which seems to have stood the test of time.

The pupils wanted to talk.

'What the other professionals taught me was bunk,' said a young man who told me he was a 'clerk' in a hardware store.

'Yeh, that's right,' agreed another. The third vigorously nodded his head.

Whatever the maestro has done to them, they now belonged to him—body and soul. This is probably a good thing.

Ernest Jones arrived in the middle of their song of adulation. He said, 'Sorry I'm late.' The pupils kissed his boots with whatever words they had handy. Lessons began.

I propose to snatch bits of 'Jones' as they occur. But you must visit him yourself to get the full, lasting flavour.

First, Ernest Jones never believes in telling you what *not* to do in golf. This he regards as important, and if you foozle a shot into the net and ask what you did wrong, he will jump down your throat with an expected flash of anger. 'We won't *ever* mention bad shots. You understand?' says Ernest with such emphasis that the matter is really finished.

Before I describe a typical lesson, you should know something of this unusual man's background. Much has already been written, so I will merely paint in the highlights.

Ernest Jones was born near Manchester in 1891. After learning the craft of clubmaking, he became a promising young assistant professional. This was at the Chislehurst Golf Club, in Kent. He went to the '14–'18 war, was wounded at Loos, and had his right leg amputated. He didn't give up golf. In fact, even before he got

"Take my wife — she's got a lovely natural swing..."

an artificial limb he played the Chislehurst course in seventy strokes—balancing on one leg! In 1921 he broke the record for Chislehurst with a sixty-four, and by then he had firmly established in his own mind that only one thing really matters in golf—*you must swing the clubhead*. The distance the ball goes depends only on clubhead speed at impact, and *you cannot move a clubhead faster than you can swing it*.

Swing—swing—swing. Think of nothing else. That is what Ernest Jones preaches morning, noon, and night to thousands of addicts in bars, restaurants, clubs, in the street. . . . And, of course, formally in his Academy. For fervour and sincerity he is the 'John Bunyan of Golf'.

If you do not immediately grasp what Jones is trying to teach he brings from his pocket a clasp-knife on a lanyard. He demonstrates the swing theory, asks you to hold the cord, to feel the motion, so that it is easily recognized.

To strike a golf ball correctly you must ignore the shaft of the club. The clubhead is an apple on a string. . . .

That is the Jones theme. He preaches it today exactly as he did in the early twenties when he strapped on his tin leg and sailed for America to take on a golf tutor's job with the Women's National Golf and Tennis Club, Long Island.

No man—even preaching the same truths—could get away with it, without personality plus. Ernest is well-equipped. He is extremely wise. He is a great talker in an intelligent way. Parables and literary illustrations are tossed in to his golf lessons to make points register. He emphasizes the power of the 'swing' by bringing in Goliath and the hole in his forehead made with a little pebble from David's sling. . . .

A hit, says Ernest, is like a Latin sentence without a verb. *Swing* is the verb.

Jones has written three books, and every word of each concerns swinging the golf club. Never does he blather about straight left arms, shoulder pivots, wrists, hip turns, relaxed knees, braced left sides, etc., etc.

All the time it's *swing*. It is a miracle how Ernest has been able

"I'm reducing your handicap by about ten strokes ... "

to write three books on this theme without repeating the same sentences.

Says Jones: 'Teachers who devote themselves to details consider golf a science. It is not. *Golf is an art.* Those who think of golf as a science have tried to part from each other the arms, the head, the shoulders, the body, the hips, and the legs. They make the golfer a worm cut into bits with each part wriggling in every-which-way direction.'

The teaching of golf, he says, has become overwhelmed in *paralysis through analysis.* Ernest is good on tag lines and he really works this one.

You will not mind me quoting Ernest Jones so extensively. After an acquaintance with hundreds of golf tutors this is the one who has most nearly left a good mark on my game. What he says is usually pure gold.

Still lambasting the instruction theories of others—particularly the professionals who ask you to 'do' things, rather than 'feel' them—Ernest says: 'How much thought do you give to signing your name? You can write while talking and each signature will be exactly the same. But try consciously copying a second signature under one written naturally. The natural signature will be smooth and easy. The free and natural golf swing produces the best results, and that comes only when you remove from your mind those cluttering details which make for PARALYSIS BY ANALYSIS.'

As a happy hacker who has had hundreds of lessons from dozens of professionals I am well-placed to speak of their methods. It would be a mistake for you to judge the men whom I have consulted professionally by my indifferent skill. That wouldn't be fair. Nice chaps have worried themselves into comas trying to make me better than a twelve handicap player. The game is littered with anxiety neurosis as a result of my antics. Instructors have cajoled and explained for hours on end, and after we have both almost collapsed—the pro with frustration, me with physical exertion—together we have crawled to the bar for ale, and talk of pleasant things. It is surprising how many of these good fellows are still my friends. In brief, I have taxed the patience and ingenuity of the best instructors on both sides of the Atlantic. Against this background I seriously commend to all addicts— particularly the chronic cases like myself with golf faults deeply dyed in their woolly style by practising the wrong things for years —the message which Ernest Jones shouts from his eyrie on the seventh floor.

Remember, he merely repeats the same story in the three thousand lessons he gives every year. You are supposed to pick it up first go. If you ask for a second lesson he will say: 'You here again? Why? Haven't you got it?'

You say 'No,' and he goes over the old routine.

This is what happens. First, a cordial reception by the maestro who looks like a genial, ageing barrister, who has taken off his jacket perhaps to move a piece of office furniture. . . . There is a net, one or two golf clubs, a few old grey balls, some strange devices (such as weights on lengths of string), and a portable gramophone on a table in the corner.

'Now, I want you to do this, sir,' says Ernest. He takes a piece

of cord to which a weight has been attached, and swings it slowly and smoothly. Doing as you are told, you are asked to notice particularly the sensation in your fingers as the pendulum swings.

This may go on for five minutes. Meanwhile, Ernest talks like a psychiatrist lulling his patient to a state of relaxed ease. After a while he says: 'Now you've got it. That's the swing. . . . You can feel it, and that's something you can't describe, or photograph. . . . Photographs are useless to learn from. . . . A golf swing can only be felt. . . . See what I mean? . . . After all, you can't photograph the taste of apple pie!'—Jones loves to juggle with words— 'You can't divide a swing into parts,' he says, '—Chop up a chicken and you'll have legs, wings, breast and giblets, but no chicken!'

After a while, Ernest throws a dime on the floor and stands over it, leaning forward slightly with feet apart. He holds a golf club against the point of his chin with thumb and finger of each hand so that the club hangs over the coin. By turning his head from side to side he makes the club swing. 'Do this,' he says, and when you have got the drill, he crosses over to the gramophone and starts 'The Blue Danube'. . . .

'Daa-da-da-daaaaa-da-daa-da-da . . .' sings Ernest. 'Go on, swing to the music,' he urges, and takes another club himself to enjoy the fun. When his club has been swinging merrily from his chin for a while, he grips it correctly and slips into a normal but beautifully rhythmic golf swing. 'Go on,' he says, '*you* get swinging.' And you do.

That is how Ernest Jones starts to teach golf. Unorthodox, but his successes are astounding. Most well-known professionals swear by him. Others just swear. That is because Ernest has often hit at them pretty hard. He does not mince words in criticism of methods he believes to be wrong.

Hundreds of Americans have learnt golf the Jones way. They have a tremendous respect for the little Englishman whose teaching technique has never changed. No one laughs at his gramophone swinging. Excepting perhaps the ghost of old Johann Strauss, everyone is happy in the firm belief that Ernest Jones smooths the rocky path leading to better and sweeter golf.

"He combines music with his golf!"

When you leave the academy Ernest may give you his souvenir cards. One, which I would like to see embroidered on all golf club tablecloths, and regularly sung by choristers on the first tee, says:

Swing the clubhead with the hands. Make it swing. Do not allow anything to overpower the swinging motion; if it is a swing, it demands freedom. To acquire greater distance, increase the arc of the swing; but never swing the head back beyond a point where hand control is lost. Swing the clubhead with both hands. Swing it with live hands. Above all, trust the swing.

Another card is a parody on the Gettysburg Address. It starts, 'I pledge allegiance to the swing . . .' The piece was written by enthusiastic pupil—Danny Kaye.

In 1949 Ernest Jones came to England for a holiday. He played some golf down on the south coast at Littlestone with Cyril Horne, the Professional. Miss Enid Wilson, my friend Graeme Nicholl, and other golf addicts were also there. They saw Ernest hit the ball two-hundred-and-thirty yards—*while sitting on a kitchen chair*.

Yours,
DAD

"Now, Miss Bottomley, I want you to relax...Remember its only a game..."

DEAR SON: We have often agreed that a top-level golfer must have other qualifications than an ability to hit the ball far and straight. He requires many quivers to his bow. The game is more than bogey-bogey-bogey . . . *ad infinitum*, with perhaps a birdie or two dropped in for good measure.

Truth to tell, an indifferent performer such as your ageing parent—derives a subtle satisfaction from knowing that although our handicaps (like our enthusiasm) are on a big scale, and although we cannot keep the occasional 7 off our cards, we do at any rate know the background and frills of the game.

Don't be too proud to learn from us, my boy. Golfology knows no boundaries. Explore it where you can.

It is unlikely that you will ever entirely be equipped, but as items come to mind I shall jot them down.

Perhaps you will decide to practise in the privacy of your desert tent. In any case, your memory will be refreshed. Not only your strong left arm may need coaxing back to form when you return to the home course. In other words, I am recommending concentrated study.

The 'compleat goffer' must feel and look the part. This is not necessarily achieved by a correct choice of clothes, although the sartorial aspect can be important. For instance, it would be nonsense for a rabbit of twenty-four handicap to wear black and white golf shoes; just as it is unthinkable for a scratch man to tuck

"Okay, old man, nine o'clock on the tee - You'll beat me easily - I haven't touched a club for weeks..."

his trousers into his socks. There are always irrelevancies. I remember once playing at Gleneagles with an old Scot who broke all the clothing rules. He only dropped about four strokes in eighteen holes, yet he played in brown boots and knickerbockers.

Mannerisms, foibles, and conversation (subject, and manner-of) can be important. In fact, everything done, thought, and said, from the moment you step on to the first tee, until you drag your weary body off the eighteenth green, should be studied with care. These aspects are as important to top-level golf as the half-time slice of lemon in a football match.

Now, I cannot remember everything. But I shall skim over some of the facets of the game, and maybe this letter will stimulate thought.

We will not waste time on normal eventualities in all-weather golf. I am thinking of the ability to put on a pair of waterproof trousers while standing on one leg in a howling gale. Not easy. You can stumble, and your shoe spikes can tear the pants, or worse, you can sit plump on your arse and be laughed off the course. The correct way is to maintain balance by holding the shoulder of your caddie, or your caddie-car. Better still, put waterproofs on in the locker-room before you start. In Britain you can nearly always count on rain.

Do you use the dodge of tossing grass into the air to see which way the wind is blowing? Good golfers always do that.

There are items of golf lore which you simply must know. If they are referred to and you look gawky the result could be serious. Many a reasonably efficient player has found himself dropped from a good Sunday morning four-ball because his vacant stare showed he didn't know who 'J. H.' was.

I can't see how one can learn these things. So far as I know there has never been a glossary of golf lore. I suppose it is simply a question of reading and almost learning by heart two or three hundred golf books. There is no short cut to attaining senior status. It is like being a centenarian: you cannot possibly become one until you have lived for a hundred years. How could a man possibly know that 'J. H.' was one of the great triumvirate if he

"They dont all go to Harlech to see the castle!"

has not swotted through dozens of fine golf books and listened for hours to senior members when they are slightly in their cups? 'I remember once seeing J. H. use his cleek into the wind at Westward Ho! . . .' That sort of thing.

'You have been brought up in this atmosphere, so the facts of golf come as second nature. I am sure that when the time comes you will see to it that your own offspring are as well schooled. One comforting thought I always permit myself: in whatsoever manner I may have erred in preparing you for the battle of life no one can say I denied you golf.

Let me continue.

Top-level golfers know all about Willis Park's superlative putting, and it matters not one jot that the skill of this almost legendary figure has increased considerably since he died. Also, we must know of more recent things. Such as 'Henry's' (it should never be necessary to say 'Cotton') two classical match-winning drives. The one at Walton Heath, of course, and the one against Whitcombe at Muirfield.

Magnificent stuff!—retold again and again over stoups of ale in every golf bar in the world, in the manner ancient minstrels repeated their songs through the ages.

But you must be able to toss in a bit of new, personal stuff. Get into the stream of history. Contribute something which the company can pass on.

I remember, once, when I was grovelling in a patch of fern, James Braid drove right over my head. When he and his partner went through, Mr. Braid nodded to me and politely said 'Thanks'. Now, you may well hear someone else tell of this incident. James Braid's comment to me on passing may have developed into a long witty conversation in broad Scottish dialect, but you must not mind that. And do not, I implore you, attempt to contradict. Spice can be added but these tales should never be watered down. Whoever he is, the teller who repeats the little Braid story has my complete permission to embellish the incident in any way he likes. Even my own account only remotely resembles what actually happened. You must give the customers value. Their indulgence is worth it.

If a chap at your club mentions the 'Road Hole', don't for Pete's sake ask 'What road?' And when the same man speaks of 'Hell Bunker' see that you shake your head sadly and assume the proper expression, as if recalling your own particular grim memories of the Royal and Ancient hazard. This kind of support helps the chap who is telling the tale, and since he has politely listened to you it is only fair that you rally round when it's his turn.

As I said, these things probably come as second nature to you. But have you mastered the practical, if not more subtle, aspects of golf? Without even partly removing the club from your bag, can you immediately distinguish a nine from a six? Sometimes the makers cheat by putting a dot under the figure. Even then you have to remember whether the dot means top, or bottom!

It is obvious to you, so you are never likely to commit the grave sin of saying '*my*' ball, instead of '*our*' ball, when playing with a caddie. I boobed, the first time I employed one. The caddie was so sulky that he wouldn't smoke my cigarettes.

You will always recognize a tiger golfer when he plays a short

"This is Mister McDowall, dear,
you've heard me speak of old Mac..."

TEE THOUGHTS NO. 7

hole. Rabbits rummage in their pockets for tees; not so the player of class. Carefully examining the particular yard of grass on which he intends his ball to pitch, the tiger casually knocks up a small clod of earth. This he does dexterously with his six iron. Then he carefully balances his ball on the pinnacle and smites it 170 yards —still employing the six iron.

Teeing up this way is a prerogative of the high-level operator. You should study the same fellow when he takes a long putt. First, when you offer to tend the flag, he says 'No, leave it.' Slowly, he inspects the turf, pretends to move a loose blade of grass which really isn't there, then bends over to examine his ball (or perhaps to breathe a fierce warning that it had better drop, or else). Next, the tiger fixes the hole with his beady eye. I mean really fixes it, with a penetrating, unflinching stare. He takes a deep, almost savage pull at his cigarette, sucking smoke deep into his innards. Then, as the smoke oozes from his nostrils, he slowly creeps behind his ball and gets down on one knee. More like a panther than a tiger, he rises, stalks up to ball, and—this is the bit

I like—he roughly plucks the cigarette from his mouth and tosses it aside *without, even for a split second, shifting his eye from the target*. You know instinctively that this man is a fine golfer. He knows what putting is all about. It seems unimportant whether or not he sinks the putt.

So many golfers are distinguishable as small fry the moment they open their mouths. This is what I mean. Your opponent has driven one into roughage where lives have been lost. Don't say 'O, bad luck'. It may be. But more likely it was a bad shot. The striker knows it, and doesn't require to be told by you. You are not really so daft as to think it was bad luck when in fact his club-head came across the ball. No, you merely said 'O, bad luck' to be nice. And that is where you were wrong. That wasn't being nice. It was being nasty, and aggravating. Much better to say 'Nearly, old chap. It could have been a beauty. I liked your hands——'

Now I would like you to study that last sentence. Every word has been carefully thought out. You can use the phrase on many occasions. Not during the same round, of course, but at critical points in almost any match. First, your 'Nearly, old chap' rings

One 'off the meat' at Ferndown

true. The striker always thinks every shot is nearly good. Had it just had that little bit of something it would have been a beauty. . . . Your opponent will like your appraisal. He will be flattered to think you analysed his stroke and saw that it contained some pure gold.

But you will remember, at all times, that this man is your adversary. He is there to be beaten. You must defeat him, so you add the subtlety 'I liked your hands.' He liked my hands—he liked my hands—he liked my hands. . . . Buzzing in your opponent's brain. He thinks, 'What was there to like about them?' . . . Henry Cotton says, 'Hands and arms are eighty-five per cent of the shot.' . . . Hands . . . Hands. . . .

For a while the poor goof can think of nothing but his hands! Long before he addresses the ball for his next shot he feels as if each hand has at least eight fingers. . . . Inevitably, his grip has changed. . . . He fluffs the next. You've got him.

There is another way. When the adversary makes a bad shot you might try a dead silence. Screw up your eyes, look in the direction of his ball, and *sadly shake your head*. Diabolically cruel, this trick can be most effective.

Have you learnt how to pick up a golf ball without bending down? A quick flick with an iron club, and the ball tosses up into the air. You then let it hit the head of the club once, and bounce untouched into your bag of practice balls. This is very clever. All the pros do it beautifully. Although it takes hours of practice, really good performers are held in tremendous respect and are invited into all the best Sunday morning four-balls.

Yours,
DAD

P.S. Some say that it is much easier to learn a good sweet golf swing than to acquire all the tricks of gamesmanship. Don't believe them. A swing sometimes gets a kink in it but the good old psychological warfare never fails. Not that I want you to cheat.

14

DEAR SON: Have you read about mass hypnotism? We are told that Americans are using it as a means for 'motivating' the sales of household products. Terrifying. Just imagine! A chap on television conditions a few million viewers into carrying out his wishes!

Thinking it over, I have to admit that there is nothing new about this. In our own little way, golfers have been pulling this trick for years. In fact, the 'conditioning' of one's opponent could well be regarded as the blue-riband of match play technique.

It is a valuable asset which you must acquire.

In the parry and thrust of those fierce President's Cup knock-out matches, we often find ourselves engaged in duels with men of steel. They neither give nor expect anything but efficient savagery. On those occasions, quiet subterfuge sometimes wins the day.

You would never think of interfering with your ball to improve a lie, but you will rack your brain to think of a casual remark which will snap your opponent's concentration, or make him press. These tactics are common practice. Mind controls muscle and we all know that a discordant note can put jerks into a rhythmic golf swing.

So we administer the poison. No question of unfair advantage arises, because the man against you knows all the ruses. He is vigilant, and can well parry your move with some pleasantry which will make you feel such a heel that you forget to pivot for your next shot. Your ball laughs like hell, bounds off into a sand trap, while the opponent snuggles up behind the protection of his wit.

What I now have to explain is a positive stratagem of a totally different order. *Suaviter in modo, fortiter in re.*

By following this closely and putting it into practice you can save as many as ten shots in a single round.

Like everything else in life, when this manœuvre has been thoroughly mastered it is simple; can be easily practised in the privacy of any room with a mirror; can be utilized by long-handicap rabbits as successfully as by scratch tigers.

Preamble: How often, when you go up to play a yard putt, does the opponent say 'I'll give you that?' It is extremely important that he should. Yarders are snorters, easy to miss, and so devastating—when missed—to the rest of your game. Miss a couple of consecutive yarders and your iron play falls in tatters.

If the opponent does not give you *every* putt of four feet, or less, you do not possess the most powerful weapon in a golfer's armoury. Call it hypnotic confidence, if you like.

On the green you must give the impression of being a man who never misses. But much more than that. You must exude a confidence that not only convinces the opponent that you never fail, but *he must be incapable of doubting your skill*! The expression in your eyes, your deportment, everything about you, must affect your adversary in such a way that *he dare not ask you to putt*. If he did it would be the behaviour of a cad, *and* he would look ridiculous. The last part is the most effective.

You must not think that the aura of confidence which hangs around certain tigers when they swagger up to address short putts is normal. Far from it. The conqueror's walk, the casual swish of the club at nothing in particular, the smirk. . . . All have been carefully planned.

On your wavelength, from his wily brain the tiger is transmitting: 'Why does this mutt want me to putt? Doesn't he know the ball can't help but drop in the hole? What a bore. . . .'

Get a load of that stuff and hastily you say 'Okay. Given.' No one likes to be thought a fool—or a meany.

If this chap
hits it — I'll
eat my cap

Before the incident has properly registered with you, the tiger's ball has been knocked away and he is striding towards the next tee to take the honour.

This 'confidence trick', whereby you have transfixed your opponent into the jelly-like condition of never being able to ask you to play short 'uns, is easy to learn.

First, the drill must be studied, then rehearsed before a wardrobe mirror. When the moves and expressions have been fully mastered, try it out on the long-handicap new member who doesn't know that, like him, you also are in full possession of human failings.

This way: Making sure that the opponent is looking in your direction, take a casual glance at your ball. Almost imperceptibly, sigh with boredom, then stroll slowly over to your caddie-car. Whistle softly (something big, like 'Invictus', or 'Trees') while withdrawing your putter. With only the suggestion of a swagger advance to the ball, but as you approach it see that *you pass in front of your opponent*. If you are careless about this he will pretend he hasn't seen you, then when the ball has been safely slotted, he will say, 'Oh, I didn't want you to putt that.' Didn't he just!

As you pass the opponent, flash over a quick grin squarely into his eyes. This is important, for you have reached the crisis point. Blend arrogance with incredulity. 'Who the hell does this chap think he is? Making me putt a yarder!' All that should be in your split second glance. Do not flinch. Your grin must not suggest a question—'Aren't you giving me this?' That would be fatal. The opponent will not be slow to seize his advantage. 'I want to see that,' he will say with such menace that you will be thrown into agitation.

Throughout the moves, complete mastery must be the key-note. Think of pleasant things, like clearing off your overdraft, the new set of irons you have on order. . . .

Now, carefully study this strategy. When you have completely assimilated the role, play it always. Even for longish putts. Soon you will have an enviable reputation as a brilliant, safe putter. At the annual revision maybe your handicap will be reduced. This will gladden or infuriate you—depending upon how you feel about these things.

Yours,
DAD

Is it worry that makes me slice?

TEE THOUGHTS NO. 8

DEAR SON: It was good to know that you have found a kindred spirit who enjoys the talk side of golf. The game offers this considerable compensation even to the dubs, and back in the clubhouse over pints of ale, we are often mistaken for tigers.

This evening, before I decided to turn in and get down to writing this letter, I had a long session with my friend James McEwan King. Mac is as addicted a golfer as any I know. Also, he is Chairman and Managing Director of the King Aircraft Corporation. Although this may not seem so important, it labels him as a man of substance and versatility. He can talk entertainingly on practically any subject—so long as it's golf.

According to Mr. Bernard Darwin, Sir Walter Simpson was 'the first man to see deep into the follies and absurdities that lie hidden in the golfer's heart'. We are indebted to Sir Walter. But I never believed that 'follies and absurdities' are 'hidden in the golfer's heart'. Most addicts happily lay bare their hearts to anyone who happens to be passing. In fact, there is nothing we like better than to talk about what some folk regard as our weakness.

McEwan King and I chatter of nothing else, and we are both indifferent performers. Goodness knows how we'd find time to unburden ourselves thoroughly if we really knew the game!

Mac is a Scot, *ça va sans dire*. He meanders the world, from Sauchiehall Street, Glasgow, to Cypress Point, California, playing golf and possibly looking after aircraft affairs. His bag of golf clubs lives in the boot of his car where it spends lonely nights. But there's always an airing tomorrow—unless the snow is deep.

Mac has been well infected with golf and it is unlikely that the virus will ever work itself out of his system. Yet, like the injections you had for yellow fever, sometimes golf doesn't take. We have a neighbour who wishes he had my fever. As I trot off to golf I can feel his eyes burning into me with envy. He knows that for days I have enjoyed most pleasant anticipation of this game and now I am off for at least three hours of heaven.

My neighbour also wants to be a fanatic. But although he has had dozens of lessons and games with anyone generous enough to go with him ball-hunting, he just can't get to like the game. He is allergic to golf. With him it doesn't take.

Sometimes the bug bites later. McEwan King was nearly fifty before the game got properly into his system.

One day, on the pitch and putt course in Glasgow's Queens Park, he did the first eight holes in twenty-two shots. The man in charge proclaimed Mac 'a natural', and doors were opened wide for him to step into paradise. He bought a set of golf clubs, and, as he puts it, was 'turned loose on courses around Glasgow, most of which still bear the scars'.

As often happens in golf, people were very nice about it. Once, on the Kings Course at Gleneagles, Mac even got a game with three tigers. What's more, they actually agreed that Mac should take out a score-card to see if he was fit to be given a handicap.

Never in my memory of the Royal and Ancient game have I heard of a similar sacrifice. Mac's three friends were from the top drawer. Of that there is no doubt and whenever I hear an ungenerous word against low-handicap players then I repeat this story.

There was the great Dr. Frank Deighton (Scottish international), Alan Sinclair (a club champion from Hilton Park), and brother Gordon, a mere rabbit of two handicap. The course was deserted, so every member of the four-ball decided to play out each hole and fill in score-cards with Mac. At the end of the round the tallies were as follows: Dr. Deighton—69, A. Sinclair—71, G.

Sinclair—74. Mac brought up the rear with an extraordinary 221 —seven strokes more than the combined total of the others!

I understand that Dr. Deighton recently sponsored Mac's application for membership of the R. and A. No greater love hath any man.

Inevitably, as time passed, my friend's game improved. Fairly regularly he began to break a hundred. After 1,983 rounds of golf (all carefully documented), many prayers, and infinite patience, Mac chiselled five strokes off his handicap. He was reduced to nineteen.

Golf is a great game. If you don't believe it, consider the day Mac went mad and had a seventy-nine *gross* at Fleet, in Hampshire. I bet neither Peter Thompson nor Ben Hogan have ever played eleven shots inside their handicaps!

In ten years McEwan King has played on 271 golf courses, in nine different countries. Astonishing things have happened to him. While on holiday at St. Andrews in 1951 he played a round on the Jubilee Course and a round on the New Course with two different opponents on four consecutive days. In each of the eight games he was four down at the turn and won each time on the last hole!

Now, here is the sign of your true addict. He jots these things down and trots them out from time to time to illustrate snatches of conversation. Someone in the bar refers to the long arm of coincidence. Mac promptly nips in with: 'That's nothing. I remember once at St. Andrews——'

The more you play the better chance you have of persuading Dame Fortune to hand you something on a plate. Playing in a fierce gale at Callander, Mac once hit a good drive on a short par four hole. It only required a seven iron to be safe on the green, but Mac topped the ball and it screamed across the green destined for deep rough. However, the flag got in the way, and Mac's ball dropped into the hole for an eagle. See what I mean?

Now and again when snow and fog have enshrouded golf courses in tragedy Mac has been obliged to stay indoors with his putter. Once, it looked as if he would be laid off for many moons.

It was during 1954 he collapsed on the course at Budleigh

Salterton and woke up in the Cottage Hospital sick as a dog and with violent pains in his back. Kidney trouble was diagnosed and it was recommended that Mac return north to Glasgow for X-ray and special treatment. Instead he visited a specialist in Harley Street.

There was no time for messing about. He was scheduled to play at Swinley Forest for the Aero Golfing Society's Jubilee Cup. The specialist said kidneys O.K. but four discs were badly slipped. Mac goes to an osteopath next door, has his neck cracked loud as a pistol-shot, is pummelled heartily, and he hobbles back to his hotel. Next day he felt better, excepting for a neck stiff as a ramrod. It was quite impossible for him to move his head. He played at Swinley, won the Cup with a net sixty-nine!

Realizing he was now absolutely fit, he went out in the afternoon and played his usual game—taking ninety-nine strokes.

Mac knows all the American addicts. He goes over there, sometimes twice a year, and plays coast to coast. Peter Hay, the seventy-four years old Aberdonian giant professional at the Pebble Beach club in California, is one of Mac's buddies. So are the gang at Sleepy Hollow Country Club, Scarborough, on Hudson, where Al Collins the Pro, Herb the Caddie Master, and Harry in the Locker Room, throw hats up when Mac arrives.

When McEwan King visits Chicago it means golf at the Medinah, Bobolink, Knowlwood, Edgwater Park Ridge, Evanston, Sunset Ridge, Itasca, Elmhurst, and possibly others.

To publicize his business Mac got Herb Graffis, best known golf journalist in the United States, to prepare an instruction booklet on the game. If Mac has his way every executive in the world who is engaged in the aircraft industry will be a golf addict one day. Each year Mac invites a dozen or two of them for a slap-up golfing week at St. Andrews.

Have I given the impression that my friend does things on a big scale? He does, but he is a simple chap who doesn't like la-de-dah. Once he went to the Westchester Country Club, near New York. If you don't know it, Westchester is about the most lavish set-up that exists. There are dozens of self-contained residential suites, indoor and outdoor swimming pools, theatre, cinema, ballroom, squash courts, indoor and outdoor tennis, restaurants, shops . . . and three very fine golf courses.

When he came back from playing his eighteen holes, Mac discovered that a valet had dry-cleaned and pressed his suit. This was delightful. Mac went off for a drink looking like a million dollars. When he returned to pack his grip he found they had repaired, pressed, and overhauled his old golf togs!

Yours,
DAD

16

DEAR SON: Today is rather an important anniversary for me. Exactly a year ago *I became established as a one-handed putter*.

Fifty-three weeks have passed since we played our Club Championship. I returned a gross eighty-seven, having three-putted on no fewer than seven greens! On the eighteenth I missed from fourteen inches and finished in such a state that had I been faced with a putt of a quarter that length I am sure I would have missed.

I slithered away, muttering that never again would I go within miles of a golf course.

As you would expect, by evening the mood had changed. A great sadness had descended upon me. When I refused a place in an attractive after-tea four-ball someone anxiously asked if I was ill. There was nothing that a few decent putts couldn't cure.

Aimlessly, I drifted to the putting green, dropped a ball at my feet and gave it a one-handed tap, without even sighting the hole. 'Bravo!' said someone when my ball dropped. A glimmer of sunshine broke through leaden clouds. I tried the second hole, again holding my putter loosely with one hand. The ball struck the little flag and dropped again.

'How long have you been putting like that?' asked a bloke.

'For two holes,' I answered, and began to think that maybe I'd got something.

The following week-end there was a club match against Brookmans Park. I defeated my man four and three, taking only thirty putts and earning respectful comment in the bar.

From this you will see that the first time I adopted the one-hand method was on a serious occasion, and you may think that this was brave, or merely foolhardy. It was neither. It was sheer desperation. Before we drove off I had killed time by putting a few balls in the normal two-handed way on the eighteenth green. I was terrible! I groped like a hesitant old man with St. Vitus dance and double cataracts. It was in wild despair that I tried a one-hander on the first green in my match. The ball rolled smooth and straight, for ten feet, dropped into the hole without hesitation, and changed the whole course of my golfing career.

For the next six outings I persevered. Nearly always I putted well, never badly. At Royal Wimbledon, playing with young Ian Marr, the Scottish Assistant Professional, I took only twenty-six putts. On the Blue Course at Berkshire I was runner-up in a Society meeting because I putted really well, and for no other reason. . . . In beastly weather I won a magnificent pair of silver Georgian candlesticks, presented by the town of Brighton, in a bogey competition at West Hove. May they lighten my darkness, reminding me to hit the back of the hole. . . .

My mind was made up. This was the way for me. I've got it all worked out now. I shall be a one-handed putter to the end of my life.

You can say this in favour of one-handed putting: normally, either your right hand or your left hand can turn the clubhead off alignment. Working at variance, hands can exert pull, or slice. Therefore, by keeping one hand in your pocket, *you immediately reduce what can go wrong by fifty per cent*. Also, let's face it, missing a putt one-handed is no worse than missing with two.

The putter I am now using was new in the early 'thirties. It has a small aluminium head, stamped Cotton-Mills, and an intentionally bent steel shaft.

For short putts (four feet or less) after I have lined up, *I look at the hole*, not the ball. Jackie Burke gave me this tip in the lounge

What does it matter?—

of the New York Athletic Club. It is one of the few pieces of putting advice that is worth passing on.

One-handed I find it easier to stand upright, with my head over the ball. It is a mistake to crouch too low, and that applies no matter how many hands you use. I hold the shaft at the very top of the grip with my pointer finger down the shaft. At the address, with the clubhead resting flat on the ground, I loosely slip my hand up and down the grip to prevent me clutching tight and to improve sensitivity. Before I take the clubhead back for the stroke I try to make certain that I can feel the weight of the clubhead. This is a must—if you are to be conscious of the 'swing'. The sensation is essential in all golf shots.

My putting hand is always a little in front of the ball and I try to keep it that way after impact. As a matter of fact, the propelling action seems to come from a positive hit with the 'heel' of my hand. If you see what I mean.

My left hand is in my trousers pocket while I am putting. Other than to hold my small change, it takes no part in the stroke. One of our lady members, who is rather 'sold' on my one-handed putting method, says that she has no success this way because she hasn't got a trousers pocket.

So there you are. Either take it or leave it. The method seems to work for me but I wouldn't be sure that it is your cup of tea. There are two clear advantages: When I slot a long one I have noticed that it is particularly disturbing to my opponent. Hand in pocket, the one-handed way has a casual nonchalance that one doesn't expect to succeed. The ball drops and the spectator is shocked. On the other hand, when I miss a short one my adversary gets practically no pleasure from it, because he thinks I am not trying!

When the world is tumbling about your ears and your putting has a suicidal aspect remember how your old Dad steers them in. Have a go.

Yours,
DAD

17

DEAR SON: I think you will have heard of the ancient golfer who, one day when he was approaching a green, said, 'Gosh! a dead stymie!' 'I thought I smelt something!' said his wife.

Forgive me for inflicting this chestnut on you but hearing it again reminded me of something Gene Sarazen said. As you may know, Gene is a jovial American Anglophile who has served the game well, mostly in the United States. He was British Open Champion in 1932 and played six times for his country against Great Britain. At the time of writing he has just landed himself a marvellous job conducting a party of seniors on a round-the-world golf holiday.

Said Gene: 'The men who took the stymie from golf are wreckers. It was a move towards spoiling the game.'

Along with Peter Thomson, and Ben Hogan, Sarazen had been invited to the Burning Tree Club at Washington to play with President Eisenhower. I was privileged to be there. We were diddling on the putting green when Gene delivered his homily.

As I remember, neither Hogan nor Thomson agreed that stymies should have been allowed to stay. But I was prepared to take anything from Gene who is passionately conventional, so far as golf is concerned. He defends the things we like. When Ed Furgol said, 'St. Andrews could be made into a fairly good golf course—with money and bulldozers,' Sarazen was livid and burst into violent print as a champion of St. Andrews Golf Course and all it stands for. It might be added that Sarazen is about the only well-known American golfer who still wears plus-fours. Also, he publicly declares that his favourite course in the whole world is Sandwich.

On this day at Burning Tree we were on the old subject of putting. Gene is a good/bad performer but things had gone well for him during the afternoon. On the other hand Ben Hogan hadn't found it so easy. The reason he gave was that he had been unable to get his usual brand of cigarettes!

Most American professionals are good putters. They have it all worked out. Even at Lindrick for the 1957 Ryder Cup in the summer, I know that at least four of the team carried electric hand-warmers. Americans believe they improve the touch.

By trial and error they have decided that breaking the wrists increases the margin of error, and this is a point which Bobby Locke has always emphasized.

Bobby is probably the most consistently good putter of our time. He 'pulls' the ball from right to left. But his touch is superb, and to see a twenty-footer slowly go on and on until it dies on the brink and topples into the hole is a great joy—almost enough to make you forgive his government's attitude towards coloured people.

One of the many surprises which golf offers is the sight of a top pro missing a short 'un. Ed Furgol, usually sound, once failed to slot a two-inch putt! He was playing for big money and missed the ball completely when trying to 'rake' it into the hole.

In another American tournament, Finsterwald, a popular member of the 1957 U.S. Ryder Cup team, missed a six-inch putt. He moved the ball only an inch. 'Shucks! I froze on it!' was what he said.

I suppose it is the man holding the stick who really counts. Nevertheless, equipment has something to do with how easily a ball can be made to roll into the hole. Confidence in a club is everything. We all know that sometimes a putter not only feels wrong, but also the darned thing can look unpleasant. I once had the misfortune to hold in my hands a putter that sneered. As a team, I knew we could never operate satisfactorily.

'it the back of the 'ole, sir

On the other hand, my present weapon—the bent-shafted job—has a nice disposition and always looks as if it comes from a comfortable, happy home. I can hear it saying, 'Just give me a swing, partner, and I'll put this thing into the hole.' When we miss there is a sigh. Success or no, I have a feeling that my old club is always a trier.

Bobby Jones swore by his faithful putter 'Calamity Jane'. I never saw the original, but I have seen the successor, 'Calamity Jane the Second'. The first Jane had to be replaced because the blade got so thin with sand-papering.

I'm sure when Bobby chose the name it was intended to act on his opponents. He must have been given dozens of short 'uns because the man against him didn't have the cheek to ask that 'Calamity Jane' be disturbed.

Great golfers spend their lives searching junk shops for ancient putters that may have been kissed with magic. The pros will try out anything, the older, rustier and uglier the better.

I once saw Max Faulkner win a competition by sinking putts from all angles. Max is a pioneer and on this occasion he had contrived a very long affair with the wooden-shaft so whittled away that it was thinner than a pencil. It swung wildly with 'whip', but Max said that the theory was right. He wanted maximum 'feel' when the clubhead tapped the ball.

It had t'come out

To the other extreme, there is my pal Butch Connolly, who lives at Yonkers and queues up for his golf each Sunday at a municipal club. The shaft of his putter measures twenty inches. The head is made of lead. Weight: twenty ounces!

George Duncan, not a very good putter, has the whole stroke over in a flash. He says, 'If you're going to miss 'em, miss 'em quick.' Fred Daly, on the other hand, takes an incredible number of wiggles, but can do wonders.

Whether or not you are a hinged-wrist putter most agree that sensitive fingers help. I have seen John Jacobs take off the glove he always wears on his left hand when he gets on the green, so that he can 'feel' better. No doubt about it, the old wooden putters were better transmitters. Some seniors swear by them even today and will not endure metal for the delicate operations on the greens.

By far the most famous putter in the world is the trophy,

competed for each January at Rye by the Oxford and Cambridge University golfers. As everyone knows the winner of The President's Putter each year is entitled to affix his ball to the shaft with a small silver chain. There are now two President's Putters. The first, named Jean, is quite full of balls and for that reason now has a sister.

As to be expected, these are no common clubs. Jean once belonged to John Low, who had acquired it from Hugh Kirkaldy. The second putter, named Fanny, at the time of writing already has two balls dangling proudly. She used to belong to another great golfer named W. T. Linskill.

Jean and Fanny, side by side, now sleep tranquilly at Rye, in a glass case specially made for them.

I mustn't get maudlin.

To return to the gentle art of putting, perhaps my friend Danny Macfie has the right idea.

'Before starting a round,' he says, 'have two double kummels mixed with *crème de menthe*. You'll putt like Billyho!'

Yours,
DAD

I knew it! – I've swayed

TEE THOUGHTS NO. 9

Lost Weekend

DEAR SON: Tonight my cup runneth over. I have drunk so deeply of golf-lore that I don't know where to start to tell you about it. Perhaps with news of my friend Willie Ritchie.

Over lunch he told me of the famous James VI Club at Perth. The course is laid out on an island, and because the land is very low the fairways are crossed by shallow ditches for draining. A certain old laird would top a shot and the ball would bump along, maybe quite safely. 'Ower the bonny wee burn,' he shouted with glee and relief. But if he wasn't so lucky he'd growl, 'There it goes again—into the bloody sewer!' No one tells a better golf story than Willie.

At the time of writing Willie Ritchie is the golf professor at Simpsons, in Piccadilly. No self-respecting addict ever visits that excellent store without ascending to the sports department to consult Willie. Along with Alf Mackie, a fellow Scot (one time junior champion of St. Andrews) he dispenses golf instruction seasoned with much worldly wisdom.

North of the border, before golf was tolerated on the Sabbath, wee Scottish laddies used to hide their clubs in the heather on Saturday night and collect them after kirk on the Sunday morn'. With sticks concealed down the legs of their pants the young gowfers would pretend to take the air by walking quietly over the golf course. When safely out of sight, the game would begin.

Early in the century, and under such circumstances, four such wee laddies had started their play at Balgownie, the home of the Royal Aberdeen Golf Club. One of the boys was running ahead to the top of a hill to see that the land was clear, when he bumped into 'a tall, fierce-looking man with a full black moustache'. It was James Braid, Professional at the Essex Club of Romford. The great man had travelled all the way to Balgownie to play in an exhibition match with Harry Vardon, and Archie Simpson, the local Professional. The three giants were strolling over the course for a tour of inspection prior to their match the following day.

The boy who barged into Mr. Braid was the son of a local farmer. Yes, it was young Ritchie, and he had recently taken employment (against his father's wishes) as an apprentice in Archie Simpson's shop. Willie had shown an aptitude for golf and was now learning to make clubs.

'There you are, Jimmy,' said the local Professional—after he had cuffed young Willie for being clumsy—'This youngster would make a good assistant for you at your new club.'

Within a month a letter arrived and Willie Ritchie packed his bag to join James Braid as his first assistant at Walton Heath, the fine new golf course which had just been laid out in Surrey.

The year was 1904.

Talk to Willie of those days. He will tell you of a regular political four-ball with Baron de Forest, Lloyd George, Winston Churchill, and Charles Masterman. I don't think that these distinguished tub-thumpers were very good golfers, but they were keen. One day, according to Willie, they were holding up play so much that Mr. Purchase, an architect, shouted to them across the course.

'If you don't get a move on,' he said, 'I shall send my carriage to fetch Mrs. Pankhurst and her ladies. They'll shake you up!'

The laddie whose broken Sabbath had led to his appointment with Braid went on to scale the heights of golf. He played for his country against England, and for Great Britain against the United States in company with Vardon, Herd, Taylor, Duncan, Braid, Ray, Sherlock, Tom Williamson, and Jos. Taylor. And much more, as you shall see.

"I don't want that one back!"

But, although most senior golfers know of Willie Ritchie, the general public does not. He never featured prominently in the major tournaments. Yet, in some ways, Willie has reaped more riches from golf than any man I know.

In the days when some addicts were wealthy enough to indulge to the full their love for the game, it must have been mighty pleasant to trot around the resorts with your favourite professional. For that particular role Willie was in great demand. It is easy to understand why.

First of all, he is an extremely cheery chap. In those days his hobby was politics and surely he must be the only professional golfer in the world who spent his days off in the Strangers' Gallery at the House of Commons! Even now it takes little to make this Aberdonian wave the blue, blue banner and yell 'Down with the Whigs!'

Highly intelligent, Willie had a natural charm, and if I am writing in the past tense it is because I am trying to picture Willie's heyday which was between the wars. I don't mean that he has lost his charm. On the contrary.

Continuing his career. . . . After a year or two with James Braid (Max Faulkner's Uncle Harry was similarly employed at that time) Willie won the Assistants' National Open Championship, and was offered a plum job as Professional at Worplesdon.

This was really the beginning of the Cinderella life of Willie Ritchie.

For fifteen years he never missed long tours of the swankiest continental resorts. With Baron Emile d'Erlanger (Willie now gives instruction to grand-daughter Penelope) he stayed at Le Touquet for three weeks every year. The Earl of Craven's lovely house at Marshall Hampstead was on his regular visiting list. The Earl was no golfer but he liked to have Willie around to chat and play a little golf with his guests. A car would be at Newbury. . . . The butler waiting with drinks. . . . A pleasant stint.

One of Willie's many patrons was Mr. Philip Hill, the millionaire. From Sandwich to Gleneagles, Deauville to Cannes. . . . They played all the great courses together.

It was the time of the great golf patrons. Mr. Stoner Crowther, the textile manufacturer, with Sandy Herd as a henchman, had splendid golf meetings at Huddersfield. Near Grantham Captain Marshall Roberts entertained on his private course. So did Lord Derby at Swinley Forest. Lord McGowan, Lord Ashfield, Sir William Robertson, the Hon. Michael Scott, our four Royal Princes. . . . Willie played with them all.

Earlier, in 1913, an American multi-millionaire named Mr. James Stillman tried to persuade Willie to return with him to the United States, but at that time the young man from Aberdeen had not played for his country. He stayed in Britain to do just that. Then came the first war. . . . The opportunity passed and Willie has never been to the United States. A pity; they would have loved him.

As Professional at Addington, Willie was right in the centre of big-time social and serious golf. Bets of £100 a corner were not unusual. From a professional golfer's viewpoint Addington was the best job in the country.

Only the best was good enough for Willie. . . .

Quiz: What is a POT BUNKER?
—a hazard just big enough to contain a man and his anger...

As I said, we lunched together, then as if that was not enough golf talk for one day, this evening I have dined in company with Dai Rees, Ken Bousfield, Max Faulkner, Peter Mills, Harry Bradshaw, Bernard Hunt, and Christy O'Connor.

The NAGS, our fine golfing society, planned to fête the Lindrick victors in an appropriate manner and I think a boisterously good time was had by all.

If you can tell me a better way to spend an evening than nattering golf I would like to know it. Lord Brabazon of Tara, the *caché* to all really good golf dinners, was there in his fine red coat as a former Captain of the Royal and Ancient. He showed us his St. Andrews medal, commenting that to gain it, all you have to do is to be on the tee at eight o'clock in the morning and 'wave your club at a golf ball'.

Lord Brabazon's red coat was a shabby, colourless affair, however, compared with the resplendent finery (silver cuffs and epaulettes—the lot!) worn by the Field Marshal of the Royal Blackheath Club. They sat alongside each other at the top table, looking for all the world like a couple of red robins perched among assorted blackbirds.

With one possible exception, 'Brab' is the finest after-dinner speaker on golf. He always manages to get new material. This time he tossed in:

During Vardon's first American coast-to-coast tour, when the master played on dozens of different courses, twice only did his ball go out of bounds—on each occasion due to hitting a direction post! . . .

The evening progressed. Tom Boardman, our Captain, told of his travels in Mexico. One day, while he was loading golf clubs into his car, he was approached by a shabby-looking individual.

The chap tugged at Tom's sleeve—'I am an expert golfer,' he said, '—I will listen to nine holes for one peso.'

Everyone liked that, and young Peter Mills turned to me and said, 'We could use that Mexican at Pinner!'

It was nice to learn that Her Majesty's Foreign Secretary The Right Honourable Selwyn Lloyd is a keen golfer. He spoke well and amusingly. Later, we were told by an opponent that on one occasion the Minister would not declare a ball unplayable simply because it had come to rest in the heart of a gorse bush. Not a bit of it. He put on waterproof trousers, stepped into the thorns, and crashed the ball out on to the fairway! We listened to George Dunbar describe the incident. Many of us nodded approvingly. The Minister had increased in stature.

Mostly the time was spent recalling the pleasant affair at Lindrick. It appears that Dunbar was in bed with 'flu at the time, but like many of us he was able to follow play on the television. He reminded us of the incident at the short eleventh hole, when Finsterwald dropped a sweet drive about ten feet from the pin. Christy O'Connor's ball went off into the rough.

George turned to his wife. 'Poor Christy!' he said. 'It's the one shot he's not very good at.'

But Christy took infinite care, chipped perfectly, and the ball rolled into the hole for a two!

Mrs. Dunbar gave her hubby a withering look. 'Well, he might not be very good at it,' she said, 'but he couldn't be much better!'

Then Dai told how one of the less kindly British journalists said, when Britain was 3—1 down after the foursomes, that if the home team won he would eat his hat and bury himself under two tons of compost. Later, one of the British team sent a parcel to the journalist with a note, 'Here's a box full for you to make a start!'

The evening passed with the port. Maxie Faulkner was challenging Denis Compton to a blood match. He offered him a stroke a hole, but insisted they play on a really good course. . . .

Only the best is good enough for Max. I thought of Willie Ritchie.

It was time for me to call it a day.

Yours,

DAD

"The Major never gives up"

D<small>EAR</small> S<small>ON</small>: Hooray! You're coming home! Tall beakers of cool ale await you at the nineteenth.

I have snatched the last page off the come-home-quick calendar. By the time this letter reaches your outpost I am quite sure your kit is packed and all the sand has been combed from your hair.

Do not leave behind the old mashie which has given you so much fun. The club should be hung prominently on the wall near your bed so that when you awake each morning it will be smiling down. You can then enjoy the contemplation of escape from desert boredom, and golful years ahead.

But don't forget, the mashie should be riveted to the wall in a way which makes it quite immovable. This is important. Your future wife—even though she be possessed of supernatural temper-control—will surely on occasion feel like grabbing the weapon and smashing it over your pate. This is a calculated vocational risk which all addicts must take. For your information, nothing heavier than a hair-brush is available for this use in our bedroom.

Why the bedroom? Because there, of all places, tempers can boil over easily.

I recall the night of a tournament played at Moor Park. Reg Horne, whom I accompanied on this day, played like a man possessed. In a not-so-easy gale Reg returned a sixty-nine on the High Course—as near perfect a performance as one would ever wish to see.

I was full of it. What more natural than a wish to share my joy?

The day had been glorious. Midnight approached, and when I returned to my dozing fair lady she had been bedded for at least an hour. Nevertheless, she had a kind word of enquiry as to whether I had enjoyed my visit to Moor Park.

Most unfortunately, my wife's simple question started me off. In a few excitedly quick sentences I sketched in the state of the tournament field, named the ten leaders, and discussed the disappointments. Then I got down to telling her about Reg Horne's last round.

I suppose I was carried away and fell into the trap which awaits all reporters. Too many details, perhaps, such as why Reg decided on a three iron for his approach on the long hole. . . . And so on. But when my wife said, 'You've been chattering for over an hour,' I think she exaggerated. The trouble was that by then I was re-living the whole affair. I couldn't stop!

On my wife's bedside table there is always a tumbler full of cold water. When she stretched over and grasped it I should have realized her intention. . . .

But bring home your old mashie. The sight of the club—firmly riveted to the wall—will give you much pleasure.

You have been absent from serious golf for so long that certain adjustments to your game will be necessary. Your eye, thoughts, clothes, and language may be correctly tuned, but in some respects you will be a beginner again. To restore your cunning and the co-ordination of mind and muscle, serious practice is essential. Additionally, a certain mental attitude must be carefully acquired. Above all, I beg you, in those first few rounds, treat the game with modest humility. Don't try to knock hell out of the ball. Stroke it along gently for a while. As you well know, gowf isn't as easy as it looks.

Great masters always realize their limitations.

John Jacobs, the professional with a copybook style, was chatting with a top-level amateur.

'The trouble with my game,' said John, 'is that *I haven't yet found out the best way to hit a golf ball.*'

We know exactly what the professional meant. There you have a statement free from the garbage of detail. Jacobs is no dub. He is a master at the craft. Examine what he says. In a dozen words John Jacobs reduces the golf game to a simple affair of hitting a stationary object, correctly.

Jacobs has not yet found the best way to hit a golf ball. That is exactly what he says and there are millions who won't be able to make head or tail of what he means. But you know. Think of John's humility. Approach the game that way.

Many say that to win golf matches you must bubble over with confidence, you must be brash, a 'killer' who lets everyone (including himself) know that he can't lose. . . . They may be right. It is practically certain that a modest man never furnished his home with golf prize vouchers. But we know that winning isn't everything. Golf is more than that. Certain aspects of the game leave their mark on your life long after you have forgotten the matches which won you something for your wife to polish and curse.

Take for instance the week-end from which I have just returned. It has given me memories to cheer me along to my grave. With NAGS at Aldeburgh. You will know the routine— Golf all day, and Slippery Sam all night!

The Newspaper Advertisers Golfing Society is one of the oldest gangs of brigands in the game. Our origin dates back to the Boer War, and the array of cups and battle trophies which the good Phillip Hudgell sets up at every meeting is as proud a collection of gold and silver as you would find in any good hock shop. Milords Northcliffe, Riddell, Camrose, Beaverbrook, and Kemsley were the main donors, but also there is a *Coupe des Lapins* which would look well on any mantelpiece.

Our regular meetings are at Wentworth, Sunningdale, Berkshire, Walton Heath . . . and if you can show me a list of better playgrounds anywhere in the world I'll be surprised. For our 'away date' it is usually Deal, Gleneagles, St. Andrews, or such. This year, for the first time, it was Aldeburgh. In that Club's long history (founded 1884) I doubt whether it has ever been host to a mob of keener addicts.

"You've no need to look so damned miserable! — what about me?"

The golf was dead serious. We played in fairly pleasant Arctic conditions, with a gale that had the lifeboat standing by to collect balls blown into the Auld estuary.

My own game was undistinguished, excepting for one shot which nearly decapitated Benjamin Britten, the composer. His house adjoins the fourteenth fairway, but he actually says he prefers badminton to the splendid game on his doorstep. How could I ever enjoy Peter Grimes again after hearing that?

My most patient caddie frowned only once—when I took a number four wood when my ball was in a shallow bunker. The fact that the shot came off, putting the ball on the green a hundred and sixty yards away, was enough to make my week-end. I felt like asking Mr. Britten if badminton could ever give him what that shot gave to me. . . .

Let it be recorded that the caddies at Aldeburgh are splendid. Perhaps they take as their model the famous 'Curly' Smith, now eighty-four years old. Curly has this qualification for the hall of fame: He started caddying when the course was opened in 1884, and has carried for five generations of the current President's family! And while we ate our midday vittles in the club dining-room, Curly (mop of white hair; gingery moustache; fisherman's jersey) smiled down on us from a competent portrait painted by a lady member.

All golf clubs have their 'characters'. At Aldeburgh—along with Curly—there is President V. C. H. Longstaffe, a Cambridge golfer who played for Charterhouse at least twenty times in the Halford-Hewitt. Then there is that fine golfer Sir Basil Eddis, who went round Aldeburgh in 75 strokes on his seventy-fifth birthday. . . . And a lot of nice blokes who have done nothing better than near-nineties and pay their half-crowns cheerfully. We met them all.

NAGS Past Captain Mike Masius recalled that it was exactly twenty years since he had played the course with Archie Compston.

Mike used to rag Archie unmercifully. On this occasion he took the Compston putter and tucked it away in his own bag. Archie didn't discover the loss until they reached the first green. After he had cursed all within earshot and almost strangled his caddie, Mike handed him the weapon.

Archie was horrified. 'I'm surprised at you!' he cried. 'Don't you know that you can steal a wallet, or a wife. . . . But *never* touch another man's putter!'

Skipper Tom Boardman had another Aldeburgh true tale to tell. It concerned fellow-nagger Bill Needham. Most regretfully,

on this peaceful course, Bill once drove into a slow couple playing in front. When, for the *second* time the elderly golfer ahead heard the whizz of Bill's ball, he sent his caddie back with this message: 'Colonel Thompson's compliments. He knows he's slow, but he can be a darned sight slower!'

Now I must catch up on sleep. Simple arithmetic says that from Friday until Sunday night I have spent precisely twice the number of hours on the golf course as on my pillow!

Never mind. I shall have pleasant dreams.

Yours,
DAD